Ontario Dept. of Education

Hints and Suggestions on School Architecture and Hygiene

with plans and illustrations - Prepared under the direction of the

Honourable the Minister of Education

Ontario Dept. of Education

Hints and Suggestions on School Architecture and Hygiene
with plans and illustrations - Prepared under the direction of the Honourable the Minister of Education

ISBN/EAN: 9783337189860

Printed in Europe, USA, Canada, Australia, Japan

Cover: Foto ©Paul-Georg Meister /pixelio.de

More available books at **www.hansebooks.com**

HINTS AND SUGGESTIONS
ON
SCHOOL ARCHITECTURE
AND
HYGIENE
WITH
PLANS AND ILLUSTRATIONS.

PREPARED UNDER THE DIRECTION OF THE HONOURABLE THE MINISTER OF EDUCATION.

By J. GEORGE HODGINS, M.A., LL.D.
Deputy Minister.

TORONTO:
PRINTED FOR THE EDUCATION DEPARTMENT.
1886.

Entered according to Act of Parliament of Canada, in the year one thousand eight hundred and eighty-six, by the Minister of Education (Ontario), in the office of the Minister of Agriculture.

CONTENTS.

	Page.
REGULATIONS OF THE EDUCATION DEPARTMENT, in regard to School Accommodation	7
CHAPTER I.—Character and Scope of this Book	9
1. General Preliminary Remarks	10
2. Special Reasons for this Publication	10
3. Things as they now exist amongst us	11
CHAPTER II.—Selection of the School Site	13
1. Reasons for Care in the Selection of a School Site	13
2. Practical Application of the Suggestions made	16
CHAPTER III.—School Grounds and Outbuildings	17
CHAPTER IV.—The School Well, or Water Supply	17
1. Character of Soils and Under Strata	18
2. Impure Substances held in Solution by Water	22
3. Reasons why each School should have its own Water Supply	23
4. Tests for detecting Organic Impurities in Water	23
5. Characteristics of Pure Water	24
CHAPTER V.—The Construction of Latrines, or Privies	25
1. Preliminary Considerations in the Construction of Latrines	25
2. Details in the Construction of the Latrine	26
3. Plans of Latrines, or School Privies	27
4. Construction of Urinals for Boys	30
5. School Lavatories and their Construction	32
6. Cesspool for Lavatory Water and Privy Overflow	32
7. The Dry Earth Closet	33
8. Disinfectants and Their Uses	36
CHAPTER VI.—The Wood-Shed	37
CHAPTER VII.—The School Play-Sheds and Grounds	38
CHAPTER VIII.—Shade Trees, Shrubs and Flowers	39
1. Trees to be Selected	40
2. Care in Planting	42
3. School Museum of Native Woods	43
CHAPTER IX.—Fence and School Entrances	44
1. Separate Entrances for Boys and Girls	45
2. The Vestibules and Cloak Rooms, or Wardrobes	46
CHAPTER X.—Plan of the School Grounds	47
CHAPTER XI.—The Construction of School Houses	50
1. Requirements of a Model School Room	51
2. Details of School Building Construction	52

Contents.

	Page.
CHAPTER XII.—Heating and Ventilation	60
1. The General Principles of Ventilation	60
2. Number of Cubic Feet of Air per Child	64
3. Systems of Heating and Ventilating School Houses	67
4. Heating Air from Outside by a Stove in the School Room	71
5. Fire Escape Drill and Ready Exit	74
CHAPTER XIII.—Hygienic Value of the School Recess	76
CHAPTER XIV.—Windows and Lighting	79
1. The Shape and Size of the Window Sash	83
2. How to deal with Windows without Pulleys	84
CHAPTER XV.—School Seats and Desks	85
1. Practical Suggestions in carrying out the Regulations	86
CHAPTER XVI.—Importance of School Room Decoration	88
CHAPTER XVII.—Plans for Rural and Village School Houses	93
CHAPTER XVIII.—Plans for School Houses in Cities and Towns	106
CHAPTER XIX.—Particulars of Builders' Specifications	125
CHAPTER XX.—Hints on Contracts with Builders	126
INDEX	129

LIST OF ILLUSTRATIONS

Fig.		Page.
1.	Section of Upper and Lower, or Underground Strata	18
2.	Section of Rock Strata and Underground Water Shed	19
3.	Percolation from the Privy Pit towards the Well	21
4.	Section of Privy Seat	27
5.	Front Elevation of Privy	27
6.	End Elevation of Privy	27
7.	Section of Plan of Privy	28
8.	Section through Privy Vault	28
9.	Latrine for Girls	29
10.	Combined Urinal and Latrine for Boys	31
11.	Section of Cesspool	33
12.	Section of a Dry Earth Closet	34
13.	Section of a Dry Ash System	36
14.	Sample of Fence Paling and Gate	44
15.	Block Plan of School Grounds— No. 1	48
16.	" " " —No. 2	49
17.	Sawed Sheeting for Foundation Course	54
18.	Cornice of Projecting Bricks, and Section—No. 1	55
19.	" " " —No. 2	55
20.	Window Openings, Section and Details	56
21.	" " "	56
22.	" " "	56
23.	Section of Brick Cornice and Roof	57
24.	Plate Mouldings. Dog Tooth and Other Ornaments, with Section	57
25.	" " " " " "	57
26.	" " " " " "	57
27.	" " " " " "	57
28.	System of Brick Bonding	58
29.	A Notched Sill	58
30.	A Notched Beam	58
31.	Panelled Wainscoting and Section	59
32.	Chalk Tray Moulding—No. 1	59
33.	" " —No. 2	59
34.	Double Windows, with Opening	61
35.	" " "	61
36.	Air Inlets through Window Sashes	62
37.	Section of School Room showing Heating Apparatus, etc	68
38.	Plan of Stove Heating by Hot Air	72
39.	Section of School House, showing Air Currents and Ventilation	73
40.	Window Openings, showing Outside Cornice	84
41.	Window Ventilation	84

List of Illustrations.

Fig.		Page
42.	Designs for a Rural or Village School House............	93
43.	Ground Plan of Rural or Village School House	94
44.	Design for a Rural School or Village Primary One............	95
45.	Ground Plan of Rooms for a Village Graded School........	96
46.	Design for a Rural or Village School House................	97
47.	Ground Plan adapted to the Foregoing Design................	98
48.	Batten for Outside Vertical Matched Boards	99
49.	" " " " " "	99
50.	" " " " " "	99
51.	Design for a Rural or Village School House.............................	99
52.	Ground Plan for a Rural or Village Graded School	100
53.	Section of the School House (Figs. 51 and 52)........................	101
54.	Design for a Graded, Rural or Village School House	102
55.	Ground Plan for a Graded, Rural or Village School...................	103
56.	Ground Plan of a Two-Story School House	103
57.	Upper Floor of a Two-Story School House	104
58.	Design of a Rural School House, Litchfield, Connecticut................	105
59.	Ground Plan of the Foregoing Design	105
60.	Design for a City or Town School House...............................	109
61.	Ground Plan adapted to the Foregoing Design..........................	110
62.	Ground Plan of a Two-Story School House.............................	111
63.	Upper Floor of a Two-Story School House.............................	112
64.	Design for a Two-Story School House...................................	113
65.	Ground Plan adapted to the Foregoing Design..........................	114
66.	Second Floor adapted to Designs 60 and 64.	115
67.	Ground Plan of the Park Street School, Portland, Oregon...............	116
68.	Plan of the Upper Floor of the Park Street School, Portland, Oregon	117
69.	Design for the Whittier School House, Denver, Colorado................	118
70.	Ground Plan of the Whittier School House, Denver, Colorado...........	119
71.	Ground Plan of the Gilpin School, Denver, Colorado	120
72.	Design for the Welch Training School, New Haven, Connecticut........	121
73.	Ground Plan of " " " " "	122
74.	Plan of the First Floor of Couch School House, Portland, Oregon...	123
75.	Plan of the Second Floor " " " " "	124

HINTS AND SUGGESTIONS

ON

SCHOOL HOUSE ARCHITECTURE.

The following are the general official Regulations in regard to School Accommodation in Ontario:—

(1) By section 40 of the Public Schools' Act, 1885, Trustees of rural schools are required to provide adequate accommodation for at least two-thirds of the actual residents between the ages of five and twenty-one years. In the case of cities, towns and incorporated villages, there is no limitation.

School Site.

(2) Every school site should be on a well travelled road, as far removed as possible from a swamp or marsh, and so elevated as to admit of easy drainage.

(3) The school grounds should be properly levelled and drained, planted with shade trees and enclosed by a substantial fence.

(4) There should be a well or other means for procuring water, so placed and guarded as to be perfectly secure against pollution from surface drainage or filth of any kind.

(5) The area of the school site should not be less than half an acre in extent, and if the school population of the section exceeds seventy-five the area should be one acre.

(6) The water-closets for the sexes should be several feet apart, and under different roofs. Their entrances should be screened from observation.

(7) Proper care should be taken to secure cleanliness and to prevent unpleasant and unhealthy odours.

(8) Suitable walks should be made from the school house to the water-closets, so that the closets may be reached with comfort in all kinds of weather.

School House.

(9) The school house should be placed at least thirty feet from the public highway.

(10) Where the school population of the section exceeds one hundred, the school house should contain two rooms; where it exceeds one hundred and fifty, three rooms —an additional room being required for each additional fifty pupils.

(11) In each room the area should be at least twelve square feet on the floor, and there should be at least two hundred and fifty cubic feet of air space, for each pupil.

(12) There should be separate entrances with covered porches and suitable cloak-rooms for boys and girls.

(13) The heating apparatus should be so placed as to keep a uniform temperature throughout the room, of at least sixty-seven degrees during the whole day.

(14) The windows (both sashes) should be adjusted by weights and pulleys, and provided with blinds.

(15) Care should be taken to arrange for such ventilation as will secure a complete change of atmosphere three times every hour.

School Furniture.

(16) The seats and desks should be so arranged that the pupils may sit facing the teacher. Not more than two pupils should be allowed to sit at one desk, but single-seated desks are preferred.

(17) The height of the seats should be so graduated that pupils of different sizes may be seated with their feet resting firmly upon the floor. The backs should slope backwards two or three inches from the perpendicular.

(18) The seats and desks should be fastened to the floor in rows, with aisles of suitable width between the rows; passages at least three feet wide should be left between the outside rows and the side and the rear walls of the room, and a space from three to five feet wide between the teacher's platform and the front desks.

(19) Each desk should be so placed that its front edge may project slightly over the edge of the seat behind it. The desk should be provided with a shelf for pupils' books, and the seat should slope a little towards the back.

(20) A sufficient number of seats and desks should be provided for the accommodation of all the pupils ordinarily in attendance at the school. There should be at least two ordinary chairs in addition to the teacher's chair.

(21) The desks should be of three different sizes. The following dimensions are recommended:—

AGE OF PUPILS.	CHAIRS OR SEATS.			DESKS.			
	Height.		Slope of Back.	Length.		Width.	Height next Pupil.
	Front.	Rear.		Double.	Single.		
Five to Eight years	12 in.	11½ in.	2 in.	36 in.	18 in.	12 in.	22 in.
Eight to Ten years	13 "	12½ "	2 "	36 "	18 "	12 "	23 "
Ten to Thirteen years	14 "	13½ "	2½ "	36 "	20 "	13 "	24 "
Thirteen to Sixteen years	16 "	15½ "	3 "	40 "	22 "	13 "	26 "

CHAP. I.   CHARACTER AND SCOPE OF THIS BOOK.   9

Blackboard, Globes and Maps.

(22) There should be one blackboard at least four feet wide, extending across the whole room in rear of the teacher's desk, with its lower edge not more than two and a half feet above the floor or platform, and, when possible, there should be an additional blackboard on each side of the room. At the lower edge of each blackboard there should be a shelf or trough five inches wide for holding crayons and brushes.

The following directions for making a blackboard may be found useful :—

(a) If the walls are brick, the plaster should be laid upon the brick and not upon the laths as elsewhere ; if frame, the part to be used for a blackboard should be lined with boards, and the laths for holding the plaster nailed firmly on the boards.

(b) The plaster for the blackboard should be composed largely of plaster of Paris.

(c) Before and after having received the first coat of colour it should be thoroughly polished with fine sand paper.

(d) The colouring matter should be laid on with a wide, flat varnish brush.

(e) The liquid colouring should be made as follows :—Dissolve gum shellac in alcohol, four ounces to the quart ; the alcohol should be 95 per cent. strong ; the dissolving process will require at least twelve hours. Fine emery flour with enough crome green or lampblack to give colour should then be added until the mixture has the consistency of thin paint. It may then be applied in long, even strokes, up and down, the liquid being kept constantly stirred.

(23) Every school should have at least (a) one globe not less than nine inches in diameter, properly mounted ; (b) a map of Canada ; (c) a map of Ontario ; (d) maps of the World and the different Continents ; (e) one or more sets of Tablet lessons of Part I. of the First Reader ; (f) a standard Dictionary and Gazetteer : (g) a numeral frame ; and a suitable supply of crayons and blackboard brushes.

CHAPTER I.

CHARACTER AND SCOPE OF THIS BOOK.

1. This work proposes to deal with the subjects named in the table of contents—more with the view to furnish trustees and others connected with our schools with the latest and most practical information in regard to school accommodation and school house construction, than with the design of theorizing on the subject. In a work of this kind, which, from the nature of the subject, is largely technical, well ascertained facts and trustworthy experience are alone of value.

This chapter is introductory, and touches on the following matters :—

(1) General Preliminary Remarks.

(2) Special Reasons for this Publication.

(3) Things as they now exist amongst us.

1. GENERAL PRELIMINARY REMARKS.

2. The Regulations quoted above **contain** certain important principles of school house **construction** and **arrangement**, for the **convenience** and **health, alike of pupil** and teacher, which **it is** the design **of the** following **pages to illustrate and** explain. They **will, it is** hoped, greatly facilitate **the work of Trustees in** providing neat, commodious and **healthy** school **houses.**

3. **It is of the utmost** importance **that the** greatest **harmony should prevail amongst those who** prescribe, **those who** oversee, **and those who** carry **out these important** and necessary **Regulations of** the Department—designed **as they are, for the benefit, health and** well-being of pupils **and teachers. Most of the former are of tender years** and attend school **at a critical period of their lives, when wisdom and prudence** should dictate **that the rich and precious heritage of abounding** life—tender and **delicate as it nevertheless is—should be carefully conserved,** instead of **being so often injured or wasted (often ignorantly and thoughtlessly) in badly constructed and ill-ventilated school houses.**

2. SPECIAL REASONS FOR THIS PUBLICATION.

4. **It is with the view to a better** understanding **of** what **is** absolutely **necessary to be done, and what extensive** and unvarying experience **tells us** *must be done***, in the matter of school** building and accommodation, **that the following pages have been prepared.**

5. **It is to be hoped that they will be carefully read by Trustees who propose building, or improving the sanitary arrangement of their school house and premises. They will be found to contain no matters of mere speculation or theory. They deal with matters of fact; and they contain no suggestions but those which are the result of the practical experience of experts, and those most competent to judge and to advise on such questions.**

6. **It is a matter of congratulation that the subject of school** architecture **and of the interior construction and arrangement of school** houses, **has, of late** years, **received great attention at the** hands **of educators generally.** Skilled **architects and medical** experts in **various** countries **have been** consulted **and asked to offer their counsels and** practical suggestions **on** this most **important matter. The** results of these counsels and **suggestions** have **been prepared in such a** shape that **they** form a body **of most** valuable **material on the subject. It** is proposed, **in this** book, **to use this material for the benefit of the schools** of this Province.

7. **Our own Provincial Board** of **Health, too, has** devoted a large share **of attention to this** subject. **It** has, by **means of** circulars addressed to **teachers and trustees** throughout Ontario, **obtained** a varied amount of **information in regard to the** present condition of the **school houses. This the Board has** embodied **in its** report **for 1883. In** addition to this **information, special** papers **on School Hygiene and** kindred subjects have

also been prepared for the report by members of the Board. To these they have added the results of their own professional experience, fortified, as it so largely is, by similar experience on the part of noted scientists and eminent physicians and observers elsewhere.

8. It will be seen, therefore, that if Trustees err in the future in regard to this part of their work, they will do so without any excuse. They will do so, too, in opposition to the wisest counsels and most imperative warnings of men who speak of facts carefully observed and noted. These men tell us that the foul air which, day by day and year by year, children of all ages and constitutions are compelled to breathe in some of our school houses is poisonous and deadly—the "ill effects of which neither the open window nor the school recess"* is able to counteract in any perceptible degree. Statistics, too, corroborated by sad experiences, tell us that most valuable lives of teachers are yearly literally sacrificed to the parsimony, or ill-advised economy of many of those who have to do with the choice of school sites and the erection of school houses.†

3. Things as They now Exist amongst Us.

9. A word as to the state of things which now exists amongst us, and against the continuance of which an earnest but kindly word of warning is uttered in this work. Mr. David Fotheringham, the Public School Inspector for North York, in his lecture on "School-room Hygiene," published in 1881, says:—

"One of the most frequent and most inexcusable mistakes of the school-room is to allow forty, fifty, or even eighty or ninety pairs of lungs to use up the vitalizing oxygen and load the atmosphere with the poisonous exhalations of the body for half an hour, or an hour, without any intelligent effort to preserve the purity, or remove the impurities, of the air.

"Too often, even now, after ten years of earnest effort to secure pure air and clear minds in schools, do I enter rooms almost hermetically sealed—with fifty or sixty precious lives languishing in what soon might become another 'Black Hole'—without arrangements of any kind for the regular and rapid escape of the fœtid and used-up air, or the admission of the pure and bracing. . . .

"Talk of cramming! Talk of home study! I dare assert that for one child that is injured by these, one hundred are enfeebled for life by the insane indifference of the

---

* See Index for the paragraph on the subject of the "school recess."

† Mr. J. Dearness, P. S. I. of East Middlesex, in a paper on the "Sanitary Condition of Rural Schools" says, "Dr. Workman [of Toronto] has made a careful estimate, from the Tables of the Registrar-General, and arrives at the conclusion that the average life of the teacher is 38 10-12, and further, from the same tables, shows that the proportion of deaths from consumption among teachers is greater than among seamstresses, and is in fact lower than in only one other occupation. If, then, life in the school-room is so prejudicial to the health of the adult teacher, what must it be to that of the tender, undeveloped child?"

general public, of school authorities, and even of some teachers, to the state of the school-room."*

10. The Provincial Board of Health has tabulated the result of its enquiries in regard to the hygienic condition of the school houses in this Province, and has summarized that result in a few earnest words. I shall make one or two extracts from this summary. The Board says:

"It appears that only eight per cent. of the Ontario schools have from 500 cubic feet to 1,000 for each pupil. . . . After a full consideration, this Board expressed the conviction by a resolution unanimously adopted that 500 cubic feet should be the *minimum*; and that this small space should be permitted only where there are such sufficient means of ventilation and heating as will change the air six times per hour. . . .

"Only eight per cent. of the schools are within the *minimum* standard of allotted air-space! . . . Less than 300 cubic feet is most commonly reported as the allotted air-space for each pupil; about forty per cent. report an air-space of less than 200 cubic feet. There are some cases in which scholars are confined in an air-space of less than 100 feet, while the least space given to each pupil is 40 cubic feet!"

11. Thus we see that nearly sixty per cent. of our schools do not allow the children even a near approach to one-half of the air-space which competent medical authority declares to be the very minimum to be allowed. The result of this and other defects in school accommodation is pointed out in strong language by the Board. Speaking of the prevalence of typhoid fever and diphtheria, it says:—

"It is evident that these two diseases cause a higher rate of mortality in rural districts as compared with the total number of deaths from all causes, than in cities. The carelessness regarding water supply, drainage, location and management of outbuildings, etc., in rural [school] sections, no doubt operates as a cause in producing this undesirable and anomalous condition of affairs. Remove the cause as it is found to exist in our schools and surroundings. We shall then make an important step in the right direction.

---

* Dr. J. R. Nichols, Editor of the *Boston Journal of Chemistry*, in his "Science at Home," deals with this matter in a trenchant manner. He says:—"It is the chemical change which results in air which renders it unfit for further use. It is reasonable to suppose—in fact we know—that re-breathed air is little less than poison to the blood. A vigorous constitution may fight bravely and persistently against the influence of poison (such as this), but the crash comes at last. No one can subsist for many years upon re-breathed air. . . .

"We do not know precisely how re-breathed air produces its deleterious influence. . . . It is certain, however, that its effects are fatal to health. . . . It is probable that impure, or re-breathed, air is the greatest agent of evil in inducing, and rendering fatal, pulmonary affections. The crowded, badly ventilated school-room is often the place where, early in life, re-breathed air commences its deadly work. Not one school-room in a hundred in this country is a fit place in which to confine children six or eight hours a day. The little ones are herded together in a promiscuous crowd; those of tender years and those more advanced, the feeble and the strong, the sickly and the well, are all subjected to the same hours of study, the same school discipline, and all breathe the same deleterious air. The hardy and the strong may be able to resist the influence of the poison; the weak and tender ones grow pale and haggard, and struggling on through their school-days, live perhaps to the age of puberty, and then drop into a consumptive's grave! *Will parents never awaken to the enormity of this evil?*"

Phthisis (consumption) stands first among the ten diseases causing the greatest number of deaths in Ontario. It annually destroys more than twice as many lives as diphtheria —(a disease dreaded by every one)*

"Improved methods of heating and ventilation in our school rooms are demanded most urgently to assist in lessening the large number of deaths annually ascribed to this preventable disease.†

12. Here are two incontrovertible facts stated—the truth of which ought to come home to the heart of every parent in Ontario. The bad air of our school houses and bad water are annually either taking away the precious lives of our children, or undermining their constitutions. That is one clear and incontrovertible fact. The other fact is, that this state of things is "*preventable.*" This the medical experts tell us is so; and they tell us that it is in our power, humanly speaking, to prevent this waste of the young life of our country.

CHAPTER II.

SELECTION OF THE SCHOOL SITE.

"2. *Every school site should be on a well-travelled road, as far removed as possible from a swamp or marsh, and so elevated as to admit of easy drainage.*"—*Regulations, 1885.*

"5. *The area of the school site should not be less than half an acre in extent, and if the school population of the section exceeds seventy-five, the area should be an acre.*"—*Ibid.*

13. The law points out the legal mode by which the freehold of school sites may be secured by trustees. I shall, therefore, say nothing here on that subject.

"*A School House on every Hill-top.*"

14. This is the educational motto of the State of Iowa. Such a motto is invaluable as a guiding principle in the selection of a school site. Every school site should be, if possible, on an elevated piece of ground, a knoll, or a gentle slope. The reason is obvious. The drainage, too should be *from* the school house, and especially from the well.

REASONS FOR CARE IN THE SELECTION OF A SCHOOL SITE.

15. The great importance of selecting a school site wisely and well is such that I shall dwell a little on the subject in a practical way, and shall quote the several authorities who enlarge upon and emphasize the absolute necessity of the greatest care being exercised in the choice of a situation for the site of a school house.

---

*Dr. H. P. Yeomans in his report on School Hygiene, to the Provincial Board of Health (1883), says "that the great prevalence of phthisis is largely due to neglect of School Hygiene."

†Other authorities will be quoted in the chapter especially devoted to this subject. See note* on preceding page.

(1) Mr. Dearness, Public School Inspector for West Middlesex, in his paper published in the Report of the Provincial Board of Health for 1883, says:

"In rural sections, where land is comparatively cheap, the choice need not be confined to one particular spot." He also adds that, properly speaking, it ought to consist "of two or three acres, with ample room for wood-shed, play-shed, outhouses, rows of trees, flower plots and a teacher's residence."

He then practically remarks as to the most desirable aspect for a school house:—

"If it costs a few dollars more to purchase a site affording a southern aspect for the school house, than one that makes the school open to the north, it should be done, as the latter are as a rule colder and more comfortless, with a larger consumption of fuel, and consequently a greater expense therefor, and in such there are more trouble and more necessity to keep the outside porches and stormdoors in good repair. They lack the genial and health-giving influence of an open doorway filled with sunlight on the bright spring days; the front yard remains damp and muddy much longer, and the flower-beds, where such are made, are not so attractive. It is generally preferable to build the school house near the back of the site. [This] . . . affords the teacher opportunity for supervision of the children during play-time; the windows are less liable to be broken, than if the school house were in the middle or the front of the yard, and the boys' and girls' private yards can be more effectually separated."

(2) In an important official document on "School Architecture," recently prepared by Mr. T. M. Clark, an architect of Boston, under the direction of Hon. John Eaton, United States Commissioner of Education at Washington, I find the following weighty reasons given why great care should be exercised in the choice of a school site:—

"Whatever condition of dryness of soil, sunny exposure, or remoteness from ma'aria or nuisances of any kind are desirable for a dwelling house ought to be still more earnestly sought in the case of school buildings, where the most sensitive and helpless members of the community spend the greater part of their waking hours under circumstances which render them peculiarly powerless to repel noxious influences if such exist. It is well known that persons engaged in active physical employment enjoy immunity in the midst of effluvia which would seriously affect them in a quiescent state, and children in school are especially open to the attacks of noxious miasms, chills, contagious and impure air, not only from their state of physical inaction but from the concentration of their attention upon study to the neglect of their bodily sensations. As the long continuance and daily repetition of the exposure exhaust their natural powers of resistance, it is inexcusable cruelty to them to neglect the simple precautions by which at least comparative salubrity may be so easily attained."

(3) In regard to the drainage of the lot, he says that special care should be taken that—

"No permanent moisture should be found on the surface of the lot, nor is it safe to permit the existence of depressions in which the water collects in heavy rains. . . . Such spots are the worst possible breeders of malaria. They should be drained by ditches cut through them in the dry season as deep as possible, and filled with loose stones, or even brushwood, and the hollow should then be graded up considerably above the surrounding land. If there is much water or the soil is very compact, the drain should be carried, by means of pipes, if convenient, to some outfall at a lower level. Grading alone, without drainage, is useless ; the water collects just as before, only concealed by the loose new material. With proper drainage, the newly added earth, kept dry beneath, will gradually settle down to about three-fourths of its original bulk, and with the help of the sod which will grow over the surface, the wet place will be permanently cured."

(4) Mr. J. Hess, an educationist, makes the following practical suggestion on this subject in the Michigan School Report for 1882. He says :—
" School Boards should always select a school site of moderately high elevation, and if possible with sand or gravel subsoil. Before the building is erected, the ground under the building should be cleared of all rubbish and vegetation, and the surface should be slightly raised above the lot on the outside of the building and given a gradual slope away from the building on all sides. In this manner a great amount of dampness and the fermentation of vegetable matter under the building, with the accompanying unwholesome air which would find its way through the rooms above, would be obviated, and outside surface drainage would be turned away in all directions from the building."

(5) The State Superintendent of Wisconsin, in his report for 1881, gives a summary of reasons as to *what* a school site should *not be*, and as to *where* it should *not be*, viz. :—

1. *As to the exposure of the children to noise, danger, and demoralizing influences.*

(1) The site should not be in the vicinity of any mill or factory, blacksmith or wagon shop, any railroad or railroad depot, nor any store, hotel, or saloon.

(2) The dangers attending the location of a school-house near the banks of a river, lake, or mill pond, are well known.

2. *As to health requirements.*

(1) The site should be remote from any low or marshy ground, stagnant water, cesspools, and openings of sewers.

(2) It should not be near any cheese factory, burying ground, butcher shop, or meat market.

(3) It should be condemned if its soil is naturally damp and cannot be thoroughly and permanently drained ; and if it allows, from the nature of the surface, pools of water to collect upon or near it, or any part of it to be overflowed by the heavy rains.

(4) The grounds are usually objectionable when their depressions must be artificially filled to provide a place for the house and level spots for the children's yard. A site whose soil is composed in whole or in part of sawdust should never be chosen.

(5) A gravel or sandy bed beneath the surface soil is preferred to heavy clay or compact muck, as it facilitates the draining of the rain water and the circulation of the ground air.

(6) Under no circumstances should moisture be permitted to gather under the school-house, thus producing a damp subsoil. This moisture not only causes the sills and the floor connected with them to decay rapidly, but it permeates the building and is very injurious to the health of the school. No contrivances for the ventilation of

the cellar and school rooms can offset this defect. When required, deep drains should be dug on the outside of the foundations of the house, and the water inclined to collect under the house should be effectually conducted away by them.

(7) The school-house should never be built in a dense wood, where the rays of the sun cannot enter the windows; nor fall, some time during the day, upon nearly every portion of the site. The grounds around the house should be so free from trees with thick branches that the air can readily circulate over the play-yards and through the windows of the house, when opened.

(8) It is very desirable that the surface of the ground should incline toward the south or the east; and never sharply toward the north if it can possibly be avoided.

(9) The situation, while dry and well elevated, should be sheltered, if possible, from the westerly winds, by higher grounds, or by trees growing in a forest or planted on or near the site.

(6) Mr. J. Johonnot, a New York school architect, thus sums up the fatal effects of carelessness in the choice of a school site. He says:—

"It should be at a distance from all sources of malaria. The foul breath of decaying vegetation, or of stagnant water, becomes a fruitful source of disease and death. Unseen and unnoticed it insidiously does its work, and spreads the atmosphere of the charnel-house as far as its influence extends. The diseases seeming to be epidemic which sometimes break out in schools may often be traced to some neighbouring swamp or marsh, or heap of rotting vegetables. Some manufactures also generate disagreeable gases, which, if breathed for any considerable time, are deleterious in the extreme. The school house should be placed at a distance from all of these sources of disease."

Practical Application of the Foregoing Suggestions.

16. I would now say a few words on the valuable practical suggestions and advice contained in the foregoing extracts:—

(1) They should be carefully read and most candidly considered by Trustees and others having to do with the choice of school sites. They are words of wisdom and experience; and, as such, commend themselves to our better judgment and good sense. Neglect of these practical counsels and warnings may endanger the precious lives of hundreds of children —the future hope of the country.

(2) These extracts are the result of careful—often painful—experience and observation. It may, however, be said by those who have only a superficial knowledge of these matters, and that too founded on local and cursory observation, that they are too decided in their tone and too strong in their statements. To all such I would repeat what the writer of the last extract has said—the truth of which will be borne out by the experience of any observant physician:—

"*The diseases seeming to be epidemic, which sometimes break out in schools, may often be traced to some neighbouring swamp, or marsh, or heap of rotting vegetables. . . . The foul breath of decaying vegetation, or of stagnant water, becomes a fruitful source of disease and death. Unseen and unnoticed it insidiously does its work and spreads the atmosphere of the charnel-house as far as its influence extends.*"

17. It is gratifying to know, as I have already shown in the extract from the Report of the Provincial Board of Health, that—

ALL OF THESE EVILS ARE "PREVENTABLE."

CHAPTER III.

SCHOOL GROUNDS AND OUTBUILDINGS.

18. Although not necessarily next in order, yet naturally it is so, that the subject of the grounds and outbuildings should receive attention after the school site has been chosen. As a general rule they do not; but the erection of the school house is the first thing proceeded with after the school site has been secured. Before building, however, the following matters should be considered and provided for, not necessarily in the order here indicated, but as may be most convenient to the trustees, viz. :—

1. The School Well, or Water supply.
2. The Privies, or Latrines.
3. The Wood Shed.
4. The Play Shed (for wet weather).
5. Shade Trees and Shrubs.
6. Fences and School Entrances.
7. Plan of the School Grounds.

19. The recently instituted "Arbor Day" in Ontario gives a new significance to this fifth item, and emphasizes the importance and value of shade trees and flowers in a properly arranged or equipped school site. (See Chapter VIII. on this subject.)

CHAPTER IV.

THE SCHOOL WELL, OR WATER SUPPLY.

"4. *There should be a well, or other means for procuring water, so placed and guarded as to be perfectly secure against pollution from surface drainage or filth of any kind.*"
—*Regulations, 1885.*

20. Next to the subject of the proper ventilation of school houses, none has of late years received so much anxious consideration as that of the water supply of schools for drinking purposes. So liable, too, is the unskilled or unpractised observer to be misled by appearances in this matter that the Board of Health for the State of New Hampshire, in a circular issued during the current year (1885), calls special attention to the subject, and utters a note of warning which should not be disregarded. The Board thus speaks of the startling fact, that—

"*Polluted well water is often delicious to the taste, and looks pure and sparkling. Its pollution is not recognized except by tests and analysis;* hence the dangerous poisons, like the nitrates, albuminoid ammonia, etc., may be drunk without suspicion.*"

21. A writer in the same Report says:—

"Contaminated water may produce directly well-marked diseases; in other cases it may only lower the vital tone . . . The impurities of the water are acting as a slow secret poison, to the fountains of strength and vigour."*

22. So much depends on having pure water for use in a school that it is almost criminal to make no provision on the school grounds for a supply of such water. Yet the matter is often neglected, and children are frequently forced to resort to neighbouring wells, to surface water, swamps or other doubtful sources of supply.

23. In selecting a school site the certainty of being able to obtain good water by means of a well on the premises is a matter of prime necessity. It has been suggested that one of the conditions of purchase should be that a suitable well could be sunk on the site. A bond could be given to that effect.

24. Mr. T. M. Clark, in his work on School Architecture, issued by the United States Commissioner of Education, gives good advice on this subject and practically illustrates it by the figures 1 and 2. He says:

(1) "By careful observation of the ground, it is not difficult to locate with tolerable certainty the points where wells can be sunk with the best prospect of finding water It should be borne in mind that the subterranean water from which wells are supplied

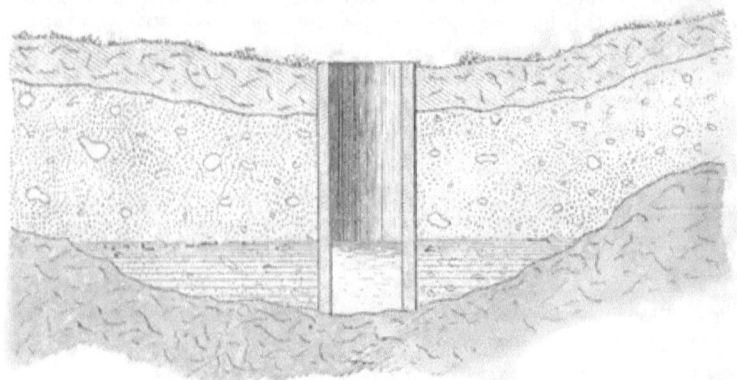

Fig. 1.

moves through the ground in rivulets and larger streams which run along the depressions in the lower strata in the same way that the visible brooks and rivers do upon the surface, each stream draining an underground watershed of a certain extent. If a well

---

* For tests to detect organic impurities in drinking water, see paragraph under that heading on page 23. See also the explanation given on page 25 (note †) of the scientific terms here used.

is sunk anywhere on the line of one of these subterranean brooks, water will be found; and the first thing to be done, in selecting a spot to dig, is to determine the location of such streams as may exist below the surface of the given lot. In alluvial soils, where "hardpan" or some similar stratum of earth forms the impervious layer above which the ground water collects, the various depressions and valleys in the "hardpan" are generally indicated by corresponding though slight depressions in the natural surface immediately above them, and the course of these almost imperceptible surface hollows having being once traced, a well sunk on the centre line is pretty sure to reach the middle of the underground channel, and thus intercept whatever water may flow through it.

(2) "A basin, Fig. 1, on the surface would indicate a similar hollow below, forming a subterranean pool, but as one of these may not exist in a good position relatively to the proposed building, it is generally quite as well to trace the course of the smaller underground brooks until one is found which flows conveniently near, and tap it in the most suitable place. In rocky districts the course of the ground waters are more difficult to follow. The subterranean channel, or *Thalweg*, is there often not below the middle line of the corresponding depression in the surface soil, but at one side of it or the other, according to the inclination of the strata or the cleavage lines of the rocks in the locality.

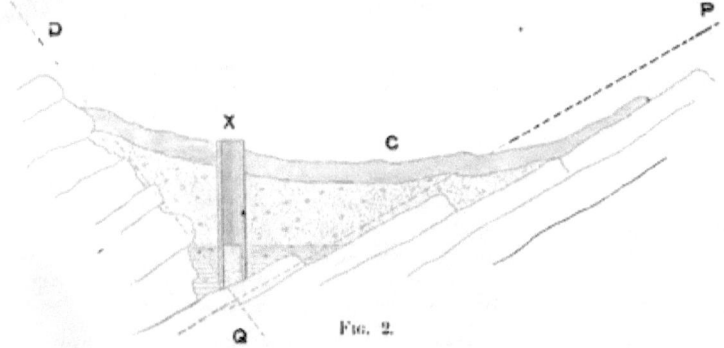

Fig. 2.

(3) "Thus, in Fig 2, which shows a section of such a depression, the main channel of the water flowing over the ledge is to be found, not under C, which would be the lowest part of the natural surface, but under X, some distance toward one side. However, an approximate estimate of the probable position may generally be made by judging where a line, P Q, drawn at the edge of the valley at the angle with the horizon corresponding with the general inclination of the strata, would intersect another line, D Q, drawn from the other boundary of the valley and following the general inclination of the surface of the ledge, which is shown by the portion which crops out, and can also, to some extent, be detected from the profile of the soil above it. . . . .

"After the positions of the subterranean collecting pools or channels are determined with reasonable probability, care should be taken to trace the sources from which they gather their waters. In rocky districts especially, impure water flows unchanged over the surface of the buried ledges or through their seams for long distances, and it should be positively ascertained that no barnyard, graveyard, stable, sink, drain, vault, cesspool or other nuisance contributes anything, even during the heaviest rains, to the school house well. If there is any suspicion of contamination, the well must be dug in another place.

"When all is ready, the well is to be steined up with rough stone or brick; the upper two or three feet should be built with hard brick in cement, and a brick dome in cement should be built over the top, leaving a fifteen inch manhole covered by a flat stone, set in cement. A well so built will be reasonably free from drowned toads, worms, grasshoppers and other animals, and if the suction pipe to the pump be made with the immersed end of block tin, as it should be, the danger of poisoning the children in their drinking water will be reduced within comparatively small limits.

(4) "In alluvial, sandy or gravelly localities, the tube or driven wells have some decided advantages. They are cheap and clean, the strainer at the point and the tight iron tube effectually preventing contamination from surface water or dead animals. In case of need, several tubes can be driven and coupled together, multiplying the capacity very greatly, but a 1¼-inch tube will generally supply all the wants of a small school."*

25. This information and the directions which accompany it are admirable, and should, as far as possible, be carefully followed. The writer adds the following useful suggestions:—

"The water supply once secured, the next step should be to determine the position of the building upon the ground, which cannot, or should not, be definitely done before the successful sinking of the well. In general, a spot should be chosen from which the ground slopes naturally in every direction, if such can be found sufficiently near the level of the well to make sure that the lift from the water surface to the pump in the building will not be too great. A site of this description will afford a dry basement.

"Side hills are less desirable, as excavations in such situations are apt to be occupied in wet weather by temporary springs due to the flow of water from the higher land above. If, however, a sloping site is unavoidable, the springs and water courses should be carefully noted after and during some heavy rain before the excavation is commenced, and avoided as far as possible. Level ground may be good or bad according to circumstances, but if wholly or partly surrounded by higher portions it is sure to be wet.

"Any moisture which may show itself under the proposed building must be cut off permanently by drains. Water flowing down a slope toward the site may best be intercepted by a semi-circular trench inclosing the upper part of the building, a few feet distant from it. The trench should extend some inches below the level of the lowest part of the excavations for the building, and agricultural tile laid, or loose stones or the common eel-grass, brushwood, etc., if nothing better can be found. The drains must be continued to some outfall."

26. The protection of the well is the next matter to be considered. The New Hampshire Board of Health in a circular issued this year, says:—

---

* Hon. C. A. Downs, discussing the subject in this year's report of the New Hampshire Board of Health, says:—"Wells to afford the best water should be as deep as possible. They should be tight from top to bottom, only allowing the water to come in at the bottom. The advantage of this form of well is that the soil is made to filtrate the water to the greatest extent, or, in the popular phrase, 'surface water' is excluded. The cement tubing in use in some wells if the joints be made water-tight, is very good."

CHAP. IV.   THE SCHOOL WELL AND WATER SUPPLY.   21

"The only way to protect a well that has not already become contaminated is by the most scrupulous attention to its surroundings. So long as the old privy system is in use, and the sink discharges upon the ground, stables, hog pens and refuse heaps are in existence, so long will wells become dangerously contaminated, unless situated at a great distance from any of the objects named. Twenty-five, fifty or even a hundred feet of intervening soil is no guarantee of safety to the well, as the percolating fluids will often go to a much greater distance through certain kinds of earth."

27. Dr. P. H. Bryce, Secretary to the Provincial Board of Health, adds the following suggestions:—

"Wells should be lined with water-lime, and have the surface around them high and inclined from the well so that there will be no infiltration of surface water. A ventilating pipe short above the surface and deep below the top of well as an inlet, and another, short below and high into air for an outlet ventilator. Top of well must be tightly laid, to prevent leaking through it."

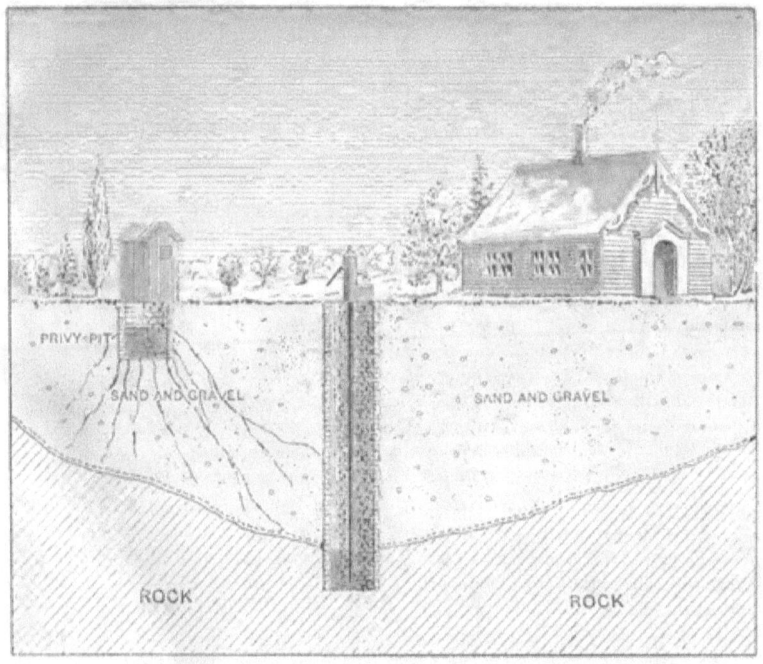

FIG. 3.—PERCOLATION FROM THE PRIVY PIT TOWARDS THE WELL.

28. To show how drainage from the privy from higher levels of a school site, and from other places, towards the well, see the accompanying illustration, (Fig 3). Care should be taken, as suggested in the preceding paragraph, to prevent this.

Impure Substances Held in Solution by Water.

29. As to the power of water to hold injurious substances in solution, I quote the following striking passage on the subject from a lecture by Dr. Bryce, published in the Report for 1883, of the Provincial Board of Health, of which he is the Secretary :—

"The solvent power of water enables it to hold much mineral water in solution, while, as we know, much organic matter may be either dissolved or suspended in it as well. . . . Waters from limestone take up not only lime but often contain the products of the decay of organic material which have, in the shape of fossils of plants and animals, been enclosed in it. . . . Similarly, wells which receive their waters from soaking through a surface soil or a sub-soil rich in organic matter, whether animal, from excreta and refuse . . . or vegetable from the decaying roots of plants in the soil—often contain abnormally large quantities of organic material. . . . Such is the condition . . . present in very many of the waters of our Canadian towns, where no thought is even taken of the few simple facts which must convince all that sewage . . . is continually percolating towards the wells. . . . Experiments carried on by the National Board of Health, of the United States, have shown that water percolating through 120 feet of pure sand in a tube does not lose all its suspended particles and bacteria.* But one important fact is, that different forms of organic materials supply food for different forms of bacteria, while the unfortunate fact remains that it is the bacteria similar to those found in the blood of patients affected with some contagious disease which develop in waters contaminated with sewage."

30. In the report for the current year of the New Hampshire Board of Health, Hon. C. A. Downs discusses this question and gives the following valuable information :—

"The popular belief is that water is purified by passing through the soil . . . while the soil has power to purify foul water to a large extent, yet after a time it loses that power. At first it detains the impurities mechanically, but these impurities increase as the filthy water continues to enter the soil, till it becomes saturated with them and will no longer retain them. Moreover, this filth, so deposited, begins to decompose, and water passing through these saturated strata, instead of being purified, acquires an additional foulness beyond that with which it entered the soil, so that the agent relied upon for protection becomes the source of danger.†

"Another source of water contamination has generally escaped notice and consideration. The foul water from many sources poured upon the soil deposits its filth ; this decomposes and sets free noxious gases, which traverse the pores of the soil in every direction. These gases mingle with the pure water of the soil and become a source of contamination."

---

* Bacterium (*pl* bacteria) very minute organisms which appear in organic infusions after exposure to the air.

† These remarks equally apply to the use of filters. In regard to the use of filters for water, Dr. Oldright, in the Report of the Ontario Board of Health for 1883, says:—"One thing the teacher should look after for himself and the pupils—that is, the condition of the filter. Filters are often used for months, and even years, without a change of their solid contents except by the addition of a large amount of organic matter retained in the filter, which becomes a source of danger."

CHAP. IV. EACH SCHOOL TO HAVE ITS OWN WATER SUPPLY.   23

"Who has not heard this?—'This well when I first dug it, furnished water as soft as rain water; but of late years it has become hard, and is no longer fit to wash with.' . . . The growing hardness of the water is, in fact, a danger signal, declaring growing contamination. The hardness which prevents the use of the water for washing, should much more warn against it use for drinking."

REASONS WHY EACH SCHOOL SHOULD HAVE ITS OWN WATER SUPPLY.

31. In a paper on the "Sanitary condition of Rural Schools," by Mr. John Dearness, Public School Inspector, he thus summarizes the reasons why each school should be furnished with its own supply of pure, wholesome water :—

"In rural schools, even more than in urban, a plentiful supply of wholesome water is necessary, because the children at the former do not go home for their dinner, but at noon hour eat a dry luncheon, generally swallowed hurriedly, as they are in haste to proceed with their play. I say *generally*, because a few teachers require the children at the beginning of the noon recess to get their dinners from their baskets, return to their seats, spread a napkin or piece of paper, and, in an orderly manner partake of their repast before they go out to play. Sitting in a dry, hot room produces thirst; this many of the children increase by bolting a luncheon at intervals in the middle of exciting play, and that, during the warmest hour of the day in summer; consequently they drink a comparatively large quantity of water. They are not often over fastidious as to the quality of the liquid with which they wash down their luncheons or quench their thirst. If the pump is not in working order, or the pail be empty, they eat snow or run to the nearest spring. I have heard of their dipping water out of the roadside ditch. A good well in the school yard is invaluable. . . . Your thirst would be great if you could drink the water after seeing three or four children standing with dirty feet at the pump spout washing their sweaty hands and faces and all the washings audibly trickling down into the well! Under no circumstances should be omitted the duty of pumping the well empty, if possible, two or three times a year, or at least just after the spring thaw, and again at the end of the summer vacation."

TESTS FOR DETECTING ORGANIC IMPURITIES IN WATER.

32. There are some simple tests which any intelligent teacher can use, and by which impurities in drinking water can be easily detected. Mr. Dearness gives the first of the following. I add the others. Any of them can be readily used by a teacher so as to satisfy himself on the subject :—

(1) *Permanganate Test.*—"Perhaps the best test for such organic impurities, in inexpert hands, is to put one or two drops, or enough to give a pink colour, of a solution of permanganate of potash in an ounce vial of the suspected water. The solution should be of the strength of eight grains of permanganate to an ounce of pure water—distilled water, or filtered rain water caught in the open, or the water-works water will do nearly as well, if more convenient than the other. If the water be unfit for drinking the colour will be discharged, or bleached, in about twelve hours, and usually the impurity may be seen precipitated at the bottom of the vial. The test is more satisfactory if a similar bottle of pure water be treated the same as the suspected sample and placed along side it for comparison."

(2) *Forchammers' Test.*—Dr. Waller, of the School of Mines, Columbia College, New York, in his report to New York State Board of Health, 1882, says:—" The process proposed by Forchammer, of Copenhagen, appears to have been the first in which this reagent (permanganate) was used. As ordinarily performed a measured quantity of water was acidified with sulphuric acid, and then the permanganate solution was added little by little, as fast as it was discolourized, the process being continued for one, two or three hours—always for the same length of time in every case, the solution being kept on a laboratory table, loosely covered. Then the amount of permanganate destroyed, or, in other words, the amount of oxygen taken from the permanganate was taken as a measure of the organic substances present."

(3) *Tidy's Test.*—The same writer speaks of a modification of Forchammer's process, having been proposed with success by Dr. Tidy, of the London Chemical Society. He says:—" It consists in working with measured quantities of water, acidified with the same amount of sulphuric acid, with the addition of an excess of permanganate, while a flask containing the same amount of distilled water is treated in the same way for comparison. At the end of one, three or four hours the amount of permanganate remaining undestroyed is determined."

CHARACTERISTICS OF PURE WATER.

33. Dr. P. H. Bryce has furnished me with the following rules, indicating the purity of water. He says:—

"(1) Water must be clear, and entirely free from sediment or suspended matter.

"(2) It should be colourless or blueish if looked at through a depth of two or three feet; green waters are not generally hurtful; yellowish or brownish are to be looked upon with suspicion, unless the colour is known to depend upon peat or iron.

"(3) Water should be sparkling and bright, showing it is well charged with air and carbonic acid.

"(4) It should have the pleasant sparkling taste of good water, but no brackish or any other unpleasant or peculiar taste.

"(5) There should be no smell other than the peculiar, indescribable (ozonic ?) smell which fresh spring water yields.

"(6) It ought to be soft to the touch and dissolve soap easily (that is, not have too much carbonate of lime in it).*

"(7) It must have no history of having caused diarrhœa, typhoid, diphtheria, or of having conveyed scarlatina, etc.

"(8) It must be drawn, if from wells, at a depth where, from distance from the surface, and from manure or other source of organic pollution, the water has not been contaminated."

34. Hon. C. A. Downs, in Report for 1885 of the New Hampshire Board of Health, treating of the same subject, says:—

"The substances usually found in water are the following:—Lime, sodium, magnesia, chlorine, ammonia, iron and sulphur. . . . There is also likely to be organic matter, derived from vegetable or animal sources. . . .

---

* Though it would not be safe to say that any water having these characteristics is absolutely good, yet no water without them can be considered free from objections.—P. H. B.

"A liquid may look perfectly clear to the eye, not the smallest particle to be seen, and yet it may contain in solution a large amount of foreign matter. Upon the introduction of a suitable reagent, the clear liquid becomes turbid, and a precipitate falls down or collects at the bottom of the vessel, in quantities sufficient to be weighed or measured. The clearness of water is no sure proof of its purity. . . .*

"The following **rules are safe** :—

"(1) If water showing 'free' ammonia also shows 15 pails per million of 'albuminoid' ammonia, the water should be avoided for drinking purposes.†

"(2) Water which contains more than one part by weight of free chlorine in every hundred thousand parts, especially if accompanied by 'free' ammonia, is to be condemned as drinking-water.

"(3) Water which contains in solution more than two parts by weight, of any metal —except lime, magnesia, potash and soda—in a hundred thousand parts of the liquid, is hurtful when used for drinking.

"(4) Water which shows more than a trace of organic matter is unsafe."

CHAPTER V.

THE CONSTRUCTION OF LATRINES, OR PRIVIES.

"6. *The water closets for the sexes should be several feet apart and under different roofs. Their entrances should be screened from observation.*"—*Regulations, 1885.*

"7. *Proper care should be taken to secure cleanliness and to prevent unpleasant and unhealthy odours.*"—*Ibid.*

"8. *Suitable walks should be made from the school house to the water closets so that the closets may be reached with comfort in all kinds of weather.*"—*Ibid.*

PRELIMINARY CONSIDERATIONS IN THE CONSTRUCTION OF LATRINES.

35. In the construction of school latrines, or privies, four things are essential and should be done, or provided for, viz. :—

---

* The same writer says :—"It is impossible to convince some people that well water is contaminated. I meet with such men almost every week or two. Perhaps they will bring samples of the water to be tested. . . . I say it is not good water. He says 'it is clear, bright and sparkling,' and 'you cannot find better water in the earth than that is.' What can you do with such a man ! You cannot convince him. Testing the water right before his face and eyes, letting him see the condition himself usually brings conviction to his mind. . . . The community should be instructed in these matters."

† In the Second Annual Report of the New York State Board of Health, it is said (on the authority of Tronnisdorf) "that ammonia is the product of the putrefaction of nitrogenous organic matter, and the nitrates are the last product of their decomposition." Wanklyn states that boiled with an alkaline solution of potassium permanganate gives off "albuminoid ammonia." When it is boiled with some alkaline solution (such as sodium carbonate) and then with an alkaline solution of potassium permanganate, it gives off "free ammonia." (See page 18.)

(1) They should be private—that is, screened from observation, or "masked," as it is called.

(2) They should be quite separated from each other, that is, should be set as far apart on the grounds as possible, and should be reached by separate covered passages or walks. (See paragraph No. 66; also block plan of grounds, Fig. 15, in Chapter X.)

(3) They should be well lighted and ventilated—no dark corners should be allowed to exist in them.

(4) They should be constantly supervised and kept clean and neat. The health and morals of the pupils imperatively demand this.

36. The reasons given above for the four essential principles in the construction of school latrines are so well stated in the publication on school architecture, authorized by the United States Commissioner of Education, that I quote them as follows :—

"In the first place, the conveniences for the two sexes should be absolutely separated out of sight and out of mind each from the other. They should be well ventilated. . . . They should not be in any place where one must pass by a window or across a door to reach them. They should be, however, secluded. . . . Yet the closets should not be far removed from the observation of the teacher, or even from supervision by the public opinion of the scholars. . . . A light and neatly finished closet, with proper provision of urinals and water tight floors, will be an object of pride even among boys, and they will readily co-operate with a teacher in keeping it clean and discountenancing the filthy habits of the rougher class. But, to remove temptation, all should be light, open, and in a sense public, each latrine to its own sex. There should be conveniences enough for all the children, dark corners should be avoided, inside as well as outside the building, and such angles as cannot be dispensed with should be overlooked by windows from some frequented place. Even clumps of shrubbery should be so arranged as not to form retreats for careless or dirty boys. This care in arrangement, so that no part of the building or grounds can escape observation, is of great value in assisting discipline, breaking up bad habits among the scholars, and encouraging manliness and modesty." (See block plan of grounds, Fig. 15, Chap. X., page 49.)

Details of the Construction of the Latrine.

37. The same writer, in discussing the important question as to the kind of latrine, or privy, to be constructed, says :—

"Having arranged the position of the retiring places with due regard to convenience, unobtrusiveness, cleanliness, and privacy, the kind of apparatus to be employed is next to be decided. Independent of cost, the question whether water closets, earth closets, or common privies should be used depends upon the [cost and the] amount of care which can be given to them. A good water closet is undoubtedly the best appliance which we have, but it involves an expense in drainage and water supply, . . . and the risk of being rendered useless by freezing. . . . Those which are called "hoppers" can be arranged with the trap below ground, out of reach of frost, but . . . [the others require] a large and constant supply of water. . . . In ordinary cases, the best resource is some form of earth closet, which, when properly cared for, is inodorous and is equally available in all weathers. The form of closet employed should be specially designed so that the scattering of the earth over the matter in the vault may be done by an independent mechanism from the outside. In this way the pulling of a lever or turning a crank once a day will accomplish all the requisite disinfecting, and the weekly visit of an intelligent laborer, who should make the rounds of the school houses to fill up the reservoirs of dry earth and remove the contents of the vaults, will be all that is necessary to maintain the sanitary condition of the buildings."

38. Latrines are of various construction. The out door wooden vault privies are the most common. Of late years the "dry-earth" and "ash-closet" systems have been largely used. (See section 59.) The tub, or pail system is also in use. The basin, or trap system, (pan-closets,) is only for use in buildings or where the pipes, etc., can be protected from the frost.

39. The dry-earth, or ash, system is by far the most satisfactory, if only it can be kept carefully looked after. (See section 63.)

PLANS OF LATRINES, OR SCHOOL PRIVIES.

40. The only two kinds of privies which are likely to be available for rural schools are the ordinary wooden—or out-door privy vault—and the dry earth or ash privy. And first, as to the construction of the ordinary out-door privy with vault:

41. This privy is usually of the simplest kind, as shown in figures 5, 6, 7, and 8. The addition of the protruding board over the seat, as shown in figure 4, is an improvement over the ordinary seat, as it prevents boys from standing on the seats. Another modification of a back slanting inwards, as shown in figure 13, chapter V, is also an improvement. One or other of these improvements should be adopted in the construction of any school latrine, or privy.

FIG. 4.—SECTION OF PRIVY SEAT.

42. As a general rule school privies are too confined in their area and are not properly ventilated, as they should be (or as shown in figure 7). The

FIG. 5.—FRONT ELEVATION.

END ELEVATION
FIG. 6.

vault should be at least five feet deep and the interior of the privy constructed so as to admit of the seats being separated from each other (as shown in figures 9 and 10, and especially as shown in figure 9). The following plans, authorized by the New Brunswick Board of Education, are very good as general models. With the necessary modifications suggested in this chapter they might be adopted with advantage.

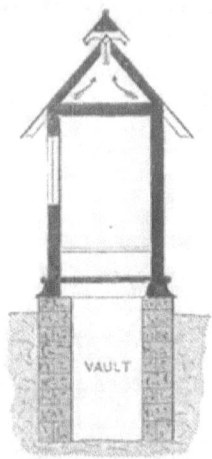

Fig. 7.—Section.

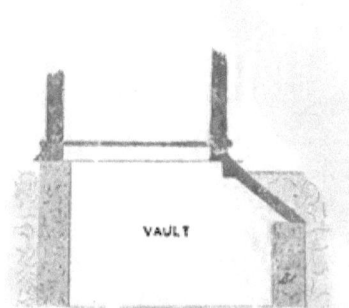

Fig. 8.—Section Through Vault.

43. The work on school architecture (authorized by the United States Commissioner of Education), referring to the construction of the vault, states that:—

"The vault should be small, built of brick in cement, with brick bottom sloping toward the rear, and tight door for cleaning out, as described above. In addition the vault should be provided with a ventilating pipe, carried up well above the roof. This is best of galvanized iron, but may be of wood if perfectly tight. The doors opening into the vault should be made tight with listing or weather moulding, and all crevices cemented up. If this is thoroughly done, there will be a pretty constant current of air downward through the seats, thence up through the shaft into the atmosphere, and no odour will be perceived even directly over the seat. The top of the ventilating shaft should be protected by a cap, if higher roofs about it are likely to cause down draughts. Unless the vault is tight, no ventilation will prevent stench from the saturated soil around it.

44. The arrangements of the seats in the latrines (for girls) in the Wisconsin schools are all that could be desired, as the plan on the following page will show.*

45. This plan is so admirably adapted to secure isolation and privacy that it should be invariably followed. It provides, by means of separate compartments, for what are most desirable, viz.: isolation and privacy.

---

* The combined privy and urinal for boys, on the New Brunswick plan (Fig. 10), will be found on page 31.

CHAP. V.   PLANS OF SCHOOL LATRINES.   29

A small window (not provided for in the engraving, Fig. 9) should, however, be inserted about four feet from the floor and opposite to the opening to each compartment.

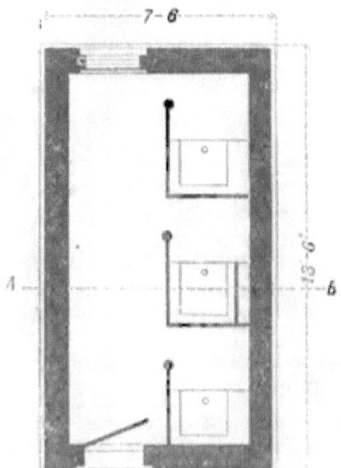

FIG. 9.—LATRINE FOR GIRLS.

46. The Wisconsin State Superintendent of Education accompanies this plan with the following remarks :—

" The foundation, of **stone or brick** [for the vault of the privy], should be laid [in cement]. The sides and bottom **of the vault should** be built of brick laid in common cement, and the inside **plastered with mortar** composed of the same material. The ground back of the bricks **should** be compact and **solid, so** that the pressure in the vault will not displace any of them. The door attached **to the** vault in the rear of each house should be strongly made, and fastened down by **a lock**. From this vault a wooden flue, without any cracks, should extend above the roof **of the** house, for the purpose of ventilation. As will be seen, an opening, **four inches** in width, can be constructed in the ridge of the roof, . . . to remove the foul **air in the room beneath.** [See Fig. 7, on page 28.] Over this opening a hood should be **built, to prevent rain or snow from** falling inside. As the wind passes under this hood, it will aid **materially in** withdrawing through this opening the impurities from the building. **The sides of the room** should be **covered tightly with** matched fencing, and then painted. . . . . **The** partitions for each seat should **be six feet in height ;** and when small children attend the school, [some] of the **seats** should always be made so low that **they can occupy** it and have their feet **resting at the** same time on the floor.

" . . . . A window for the admission **of** light, **and, if possible, so** situated that **sunshine will enter** the room some **portion of each** day, **should be** included. For the **boys' outhouse,** urinals should be constructed **in the room** . . . [See Fig. 10 on page 31]. **In both** outhouses, conveniences **should be** supplied [in the form shown in Fig. 9 **above] for the** isolation and comparative **seclusion** of the children, particularly the **delicate and nervous ones."**

47. The Committee of the Ontario Public School Teachers' Association (Inspectors' Section), to which the subject of school house construction was recently referred by the Minister of Education, reported as follows on this matter :—

"Owing to the difficulty of getting [privies] cleaned, a deep pit, well ventilated, is preferred. See Mr. Inspector Fotheringham's plan."

48. Mr. Fotheringham's " plan " is thus given, as follows :—

"From the almost universal neglect to clean the boxes and shallow cess-pools of privies, I am inclined to recommend the adoption of stone receptacles of five or six feet depth, with sloping seats at about 35° to 40° angle, with open space at the top of the seat leading into the open air through the roof or under the eaves. The decomposition at this depth is so gradual as to be much less offensive than from shallow receptacles.

"Privies are almost always too small, and seldom have urinals for boys. Both defects are the chief causes of violations of propriety in their use."

49. Dr. J. J. Wadsworth, Public School Inspector, County of Norfolk, in his remarks on this subject, says :—

"Boys' privies should have board inclined over seats so as to prevent standing on them. [See Fig. 4, page 27.] If large there should be separate stalls in each privy. [See Fig. 9, page 29.] All privies should be masked by tight board fences."

50. Mr. F. Burrows, Public School Inspector, Counties of Lennox and Addington, says :—

"These necessary buildings [privies] should be strongly made, and provided with ventilating chimneys. Any paint used on them should be mixed with coarse sand to prevent scribbling. To prevent the wetting of the seats urinals should be provided. The urinals might be placed within a board screen built around the privies."

51. Mr. J. McBrien, Public School Inspector, County of Ontario, says— speaking of the projecting part of the pit, or vault—(see the New Brunswick plan, Fig. 8, page 28) :—

"There should be an outside entrance to it, dug down, like an outside door to some cellars, with a track laid in it. A vessel constructed on wheels could be drawn up this once a week," etc.

52. In regard to this suggestion, the work on Rural School Architecture authorized by the United States Commissioner of Education says (speaking of the dry earth closets) :—

"The vault may, with advantage, consist of light plank boxes on wheels, so as to be easily rolled out for emptying," etc.

Construction of Urinal for Boys.

53. All experienced writers on privy construction are agreed as to the necessity of urinals being provided for boys. A plan for them has been authorized by the New Brunswick Board of Education which might be

CHAP. V.   COMBINED URINAL AND LATRINE.   31

adopted with advantage. It is as follows, and combines, as will be seen in Fig. 10, a well arranged latrine for boys, which, if constructed on the plan shown in Fig. 9, page 29, would be greatly improved*:—

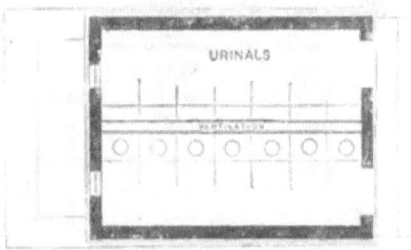

FIG. 10.—COMBINED URINAL AND LATRINE FOR BOYS.

54. In regard to the best construction of these urinals the Report on Education for 1884, of the State of Massachusetts, contains the following directions on the subject given by Dr. F. Lincoln, of Boston:—

"The neatest form of urinal is a continuous upright surface of oiled slate, with a platform of slate (not too narrow). The platform ought to be sunk to the level of the rest of the floor to facilitate the escape of water from the hose or bucket—which should be used daily in any case. If there is no sprinkling tube to wet the slate constantly, the surfaces should be washed as often as may be necessary. The floor of the apartment should be of stone slabs; not of brick or ordinary cement."

55. The authorized work on School Architecture of the United States Commissioner of Education says:—

"Urinals become exceedingly offensive unless well looked after. Wherever possible, they should have floor and partitions of slate or marble, for easy washing, and should in any case be in a well aired place. A piece of common bar soap is often placed in urinals to lessen the odour from them, and is of considerable value.

56. In an article in the Report of the Provincial Board of Health for 1883 it is stated that—

"Urinals become offensive through want of proper provision for preventing the incrustation of them with deposits from the urine, and of proper means of frequently cleansing or removing surfaces which collect the droppings. A tray of ashes or sawdust in front of, and beneath, the urinal will meet this latter requirement, the contents of the tray being frequently changed. For the first mentioned cause of offensiveness, it seems necessary to have a flow of water washing the urinal, whilst in use. Disinfectant contrivances should also be used."†

---

* The approved plan of a privy for girls (Fig. 9) will be found on page 29. It should also be adopted for boys' privies for the reasons given above.

† For information in regard to disinfectants and their uses, see page 36.

School Lavatories and their Construction.

57. Although lavatories have not hitherto, as a general rule, been considered essential in ordinary rural schools, yet they are very desirable on many accounts, especially where numbers congregate and out door plays abound. They are easy of construction, care being taken to have the escape pipe carefully fitted to the basin and to the drainage pipe. As to how this drainage should be disposed of, the United States book on School Architecture, already quoted, says:—

"The sink or wash basin in a school will give no trouble if drained into a separate 'dry well,' consisting of a pit some 2 or 3 barrels in capacity, filled with loose stones and sodded over; or, still better, a line of 50 to 100 feet of soil tile, laid end to end, about a foot below the surface of the ground, and the joints well covered before filling up the trench."

Cesspool for Lavatory Water and Privy Overflow.

58. In cities and towns, provision should be made for drainage or overflow from the school privy into the street sewer. In rural sections it may be necessary to take this overflow into a cesspool. In that case it may be convenient to let the water from the school lavatory flow into the same cesspool. But in such case a trap would be necessary on the pipe leading from the lavatory into the cesspool, so as to prevent the inflow of poisonous gas.* The United States work on School Architecture points out that:—

"The best cesspool is a tight tank of brickwork in cement, with brick or concrete bottom and a stone top set in cement. The stone cover may, with advantage, have a common iron pump fixed in it, by means of which the contents of the tank may be pumped out whenever required with the least trouble.

"In addition, the cesspool cover should be drilled with a number of holes for admission of air. If the tank is far from the building, it is best to put a trap in the drain pipe, near the house wall. In this case, there will be a constant small effluvium from the cesspool, but, unless it is too large, not enough to reach the building. If space is restricted, the drain pipe should be without a trap and the soil pipes carried well up above the roof. Then the natural warmth of soil pipes and cesspool will cause an upward flow in the now unobstructed line of pipe, the air being drawn in through the holes in the stone cover instead of issuing therefrom, and will be discharged harmlessly into the upper air.

"An overflow is usually necessary to any tight cesspool which is in danger of being neglected. This may be carried to a small dry well or other outlet, where its offensiveness will do as little harm as possible.

---

* The United States book on School Architecture has a strong word of advice and warning on this matter. It says:—"On no account must the waste pipe empty into the privy vault. By such carelessness will not only foul gases be poured into the vestibules, wardrobes, and school room, but the admixture of water renders the contents of the vault doubly offensive and dangerous." See part of chapter—on vestibules and wardrobes—on page 46.

"In many places these dry wells or leaching cesspools will for economy's sake be employed to do the whole work, regardless of the gradual poisoning of the subsoil inseparable from their use. Even in this case, it is well to remember that a small brick tank for first receiving the drainage and allowing it to settle and dissolve is of much value in preventing the clogging of the soil around the leaching pit."

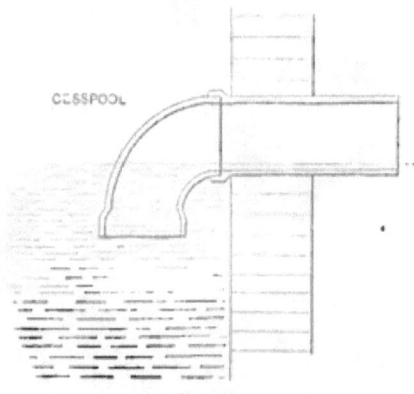

Fig. 11.

"The overflow pipe should be built into the wall about half its diameter below the inlet pipe, and a quarter bend should be previously cemented in, so that when set this will dip below the surface of the liquid in the cesspool. (Fig. 11.) By this means the scum and paper which always floats on the top will be prevented from entering and choking the overflow pipe."

The Dry Earth Closet.

59. By common consent, the dry earth closet system for school latrines is preferred as the cleanest, healthiest and most satisfactory. The United States work on School Architecture says of it:—

"Earth closets, which will in the majority of cases form the most available appliance, differ only from a well arranged privy in the fittings by which at intervals a small quantity of sifted dry earth is thrown on the matter in the vault. A very small quantity, if evenly spread, acts as a complete disinfectant, and earth closets are nearly as free from offence as the best water closets—much more so than inferior ones—with the advantages of simplicity, cheapness, and availability in cold weather. . . .

"What is needed is a capacious reservoir for the dried earth, a measurer to receive from the reservoir a certain small quantity, and a means of throwing out the earth contained in the measurer at will in a uniform sheet over the vault, after which operation another given dose should fall into the measurer, to be ready for the next operation.'"

60. The following is suggested in that work as the plan of the earth closet :—

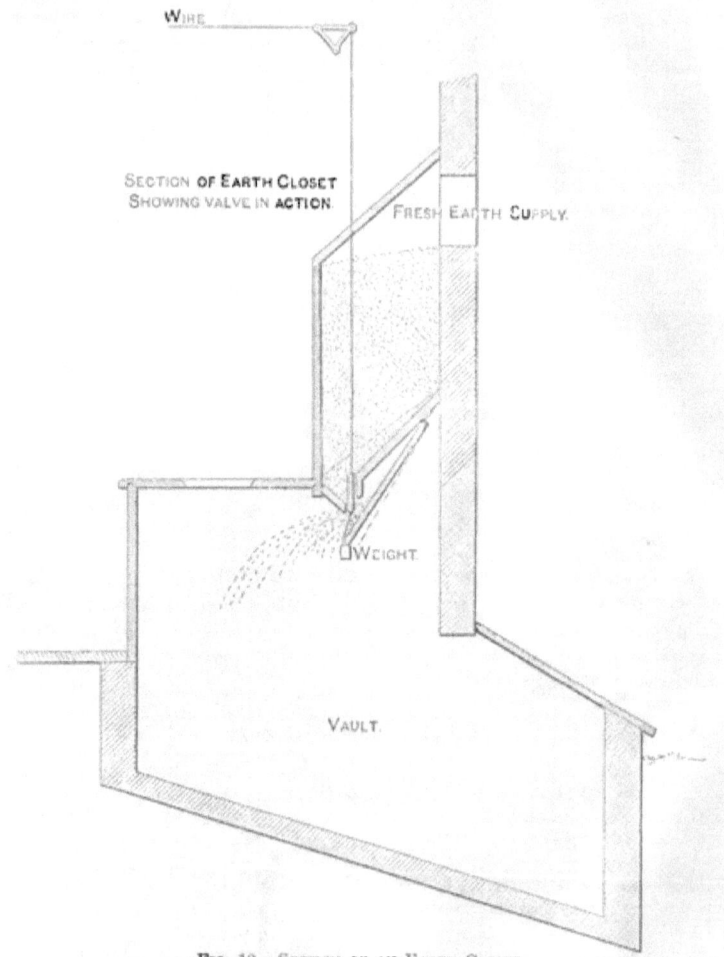

Fig. 12.—Section of an Earth Closet.

61. In this figure (12)—

"The reservoir, or hopper, is filled by a shovel from the outside through the opening on the right hand side. A lid of plain boards is hinged to the back of the hopper. . . . By pushing in a lever, pulling a cord, the inverted lid is thrown forward, as shown in the foregoing figure, and the slide raised shutting off the descent of the earth from the hopper above into the measurer, but throwing the portion already contained in it over the vault in a uniform sheet. On the relaxing of the impulse, the weight draws the slide back and supplies the measurer with a fresh dose. By regulating the front edge of the measurer the sheet of earth may be directed as required. There is a sheet of wire netting fixed in the hopper, which serves to sift the earth and prevent it from packing so firmly in the bottom as to impede the movement of the measurer. The jar communicated to the apparatus shakes down the earth, a matter of some importance. Very possibly there may be better modes of accomplishing the same result; the writer merely suggests this as illustrating the end to be attained and the simplicity of means desirable.

"The vault may, with advantage, consist of tight plank boxes on wheels, so as to be easily rolled out for emptying. If this is impracticable, a shallow pit lined with 8-inch brick-work in cement, and with bottom of bricks on edge, also laid in cement, is necessary, and for facility of cleaning, the bottom may slope outward. The vault should be accessible from the outside, but closed by strong and tight doors with lock and key.

"The earth used in these closets should be loam or clay, not sand. It should be dried in the sun or by a fire, sifted, and stored in a dry place. The screen for sifting should have about three meshes to the inch; and coal ashes, similarly sifted, may be added to the mixture in quantity equal to the earth without harm. Wood ashes or lime should not be used.

"The earth taken out of the vaults may be dried and used over again indefinitely. It retains no trace of the organic matter which it has helped to decompose. The quantity required may be easily calculated. About 1½ pints, or 2½ pounds, of average earth per closet will generally be enough for each discharge, supposing these to take place four or five times daily; and the capacity of the reservoir divided by this will give the length of the interval between successive fillings. If several relays of earth are dried and stored in barrels, there need be no interruption to the working of the apparatus."

62. The paper of the Provincial Board of Health on this subject says:—

"The earths best adapted for the purpose are moulds and loams. Pure sand is said to possess little or no deodorizing power, while pure clay is difficult to bring into the properly powdery condition, and has a tendency to absorb too much water.

"It is not necessary that the earth should be absolutely dry; the drying that it receives from exposure to the atmosphere being sufficient. For use it must be free from lumps and in a powdery condition. This is best effected by screening it.

"After being used it may be placed in a barrel, where it will undergo a slight heating and fermentation, after which it may be thrown out on the floor of the shed and exposed to the air in order to dry, and may then be used again. It is said that this process may be repeated ten or a dozen times with the same earth before it becomes offensive. This, however, is not recommended, especially in a country like ours, unless for the manurial value of the product; but it shows the value of dry earth as an absorbent and deodorizer. Anthracite coal ashes have been found to answer in this respect fully as well as loam. . . . .

"Some excellent automatic earth closets, not very extravagant in price, are, however, made in this Province. The addresses of various manufacturers of them may be obtained on application to the Secretary of this Board."

63. Should the dry ash system be adopted the privy can be constructed as shown in figure 13,* which, on the whole, seems preferable in its plan

---

* Taken from the second report of the New York State Board of Health, 1884, page 156.

and arrangement to that of figure 12. However, both are given as both have been in successful use. In figure 13 the reservoir and hopper for ashes and disinfectants are behind the seat—the back of which inclines inwards. L is a lever, which, when pushed or pulled back to L', opens a

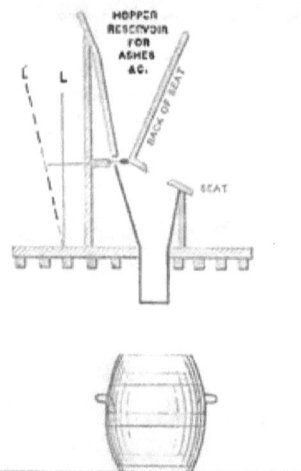

FIG. 13.—SECTION OF DRY ASH SYSTEM.

valve and discharges ashes, through an opening in the floor into a barrel underneath. The valve may be made to work automatically by a special arrangement when constructing the seat.

DISINFECTANTS AND THEIR USES.*

64. The report of the New Hampshire State Board of Health for 1885 says, by way of caution:—

"According to a high authority 'a disinfectant is an agent capable of destroying the infective power of infectious material.' Infectious material is something that has power to communicate disease to persons. Now anything which will destroy that power is a disinfectant. According to recent most rigid and exact tests chlorine, bromine, and iodine are really disinfectants. But 'they are not suitable as disinfectants for popular use.' . . . Chloride of lime, permanganate of potash and corrosive sublimates are recommended as excellent disinfectants; but they are not innocent

---

* The following definitions and remarks may be found useful:—

(1) *Disinfectants*.—Substances which destroy smells and their poisons by acting chemically; substances (as above) which destroy infections or infectious matter.

(2) *Disinfection* is the destruction of poisons of infectious or contagious diseases.

(3) *Deodorizers*.—Substances which destroy smells. They are not necessarily disinfectants, and do not necessarily have an odour.

(4) *Disinfection* cannot compensate for want of cleanliness nor want of ventilation.

drugs to have about in jugs and boxes, knowing the propensity of persons to misplace, mislabel and swallow poisons." . . .

65. In speaking of disinfectants and how to use them, it is well to remember that such common disinfectants, as chloride of lime and sulphur, are often used in a way to render them perfectly useless. Chloride of lime, prepared and used as given below, is one of the best disinfectants known, since it destroys disease germs very quickly :—

(1) *Chloride of Lime.*—For a free and general use in privy vaults, sewers, etc., the following is one of the cheapest and most effective disinfectants and germicides available for general use* :—

Chloride of lime (bleaching powder) one pound; water, four gallons. Mix well—cost, much less than a dollar a barrel. A quart or more a day may be used in an offensive vault. When chloride of lime is spread on trays or dishes in a room, it cleanses and deodorizes. It may be sprinkled over floors or passages, and after a day or two, be washed off.

(2) *Rock Sulphur* (brimstone).—For fumigation it should be used in a tightly closed school room. It should be placed on an iron pan, supported on bricks, placed in wash tubs containing a little water and set on fire by means of hot coals or a spoonful of alcohol. For a room ten feet square two pounds of sulphur would be required, and so on in proportion. The room should remain closed for twenty-four hours.

(3) *Sulphate of Iron* (copperas) dissolved in water, in the proportion of one and a half gallons, for night soil in privies, sewers, etc.

(4) *Solution of Chloride of Zinc,* when diluted with water and poured into drains, sewers and privies, destroys offensive odours.

(5) *Carbolic Acid,* diluted with about thirty parts of water and sprinkled where required, arrests the process of decay.

NOTE.—The foregoing list of disinfectants with directions as to their use is taken from the recent Reports of Boards of Health—Ontario, New York, New Hampshire, etc., already quoted in this book.

CHAPTER VI.

THE WOOD-SHED.

66. The wood-shed might be placed for convenience of access at the back of the school house.† The better place, from a sanitary point of view,

---

* "In the laboratory experiments now being made at the Johns Hopkins University. . . . this solution has been found to be rapid in its action, readily destroying germs which possess the greatest tenacity of life,—*Bacillus subtilis* and *B. anthrocis* as well as their spores." N. H. State Board Report, 1885.

† If this plan be adopted the shed should be so constructed that the rear passage for pupils should not be through it but alongside of it, as shown in plan of a school house inserted near the close of this book.

is at the rear of the school lot, with a privy at each end of it (see plan on page 37, figure 15). The advantage of this plan would be that the privies could be under the same roof as the wood shed and thus save expense in construction. They should be kept apart, and a double covered way should be constructed to the shed which, with a thick and well boarded partition, would effectually separate the passages to the privies from each other—which is most desirable. The boys' passage could be used for conveying wood to the school house. Care should, however, be taken to isolate the girls' privy from the end of the wood shed by a thick partition or a space of about twelve inches so that no communication can possibly take place with it from that end of the wood shed. This, although a comparatively economical plan, is not so good a one as to isolate the privies entirely, as shown in figure 15, page 49. The size of the wood shed must be determined by circumstances.

CHAPTER VII.

THE SCHOOL PLAY SHEDS AND GROUNDS.

67. No school should be without a comfortable play shed for wet weather, and for young children in the heat of the summer day. The play-shed might be placed at the sides of the separate play grounds for boys and girls. They would thus be placed apart from each other and the boys and girls would then be free to enjoy their play hours without interruption or annoyance from each other, or from any unruly pupils of the school. The girls' play ground might have one or two shade trees in it, and a few bench seats around the shade trees. (See figure 15 in Chapter X.)

68. Some school authorities recommend that play grounds should not have any shade trees in them for reasons given. The United States work on School Architecture summarizes these reasons as follows:—

"However the play ground may be situated, it is best left clear, without interruption by trees or shrubs. These are only in the way of the children's sports, and they soon get mangled and broken by thoughtlessness or accident; their shade is of no use in such a place, and they are liable to be used as screens to conceal doubtful actions from the eye of the teacher, whose vigilance it is well that the pupils should never be sure of escaping."

69. In regard to the necessity for play grounds within the school site, the State Superintendent of Wisconsin in his last report, makes these suggestions:—

1. "Two spaces should be assigned to the play yards—one for the boys and one for the girls. When a school maintains a primary [or Kindergarten] department, a portion of the grounds should be set apart for its small children.

2. "The idea which should govern in the case [of play grounds] is to secure space not for mere amusement, but for proper physical exercises by both sexes. No children in any school should be compelled to go into the highway [apart from the danger from passing vehicles and cattle] or on private grounds for their plays or recreation. . . .

3. "The play grounds should never be paved with stone or brick, nor covered with plank or coarse gravel. The grass should be allowed to grow upon them as thickly as possible with their use by the children. Sometimes it is an advantage to spread a layer of fine sand upon them when the soil has been hardened in the frequent plays."

4. "It is very essential that all portions of the play yards should be seen from the windows of the main school-rooms. . . . ."

70. This suggestion as to the surface of the play ground is endorsed in the work sanctioned by the United States Commissioner on **School Architecture**. It says :—

"The ground should be grassed over with the closest and thickest turf possible. . . . Whenever the natural sod is good, it is best to leave it intact, as a thick sod is of slow growth. If new grading is necessary . . . all the loam accessible should be spread upon the surface . . . and the whole should be thickly sown with red-tap grass, with a little admixture of white clover."

NOTE.—(For a reference to "school recess, see paragraph No. 131. See, especially, paragraph 140, section (4), in regard to the increased desire for playgrounds as an indication of public liberality in respect to schools.)

CHAPTER VIII.

SHADE TREES AND SHRUBS.

"3. *The school grounds should be properly levelled and drained, planted with shade trees . . . ."—Regulations, 1885.*

"302. *The first Friday in May should be set apart by the trustees of every rural school and incorporated village for the purpose of planting shade trees, making flower beds and otherwise improving and beautifying the school grounds."—Ibid.* *

---

* Speaking on the subject of Arbor Day in the United States, Hon. John Eaton remarks:— " In several States of the American Union, however, there is a growing disposition among school officers to avail themselves of this effective means of culture and to foster a spirit in the community which will facilitate the operation of laws passed for the encouragement of tree planting and the protection of trees ; in Connecticut, especially, the late energetic Secretary of the State Board of Education, Hon. B. G. Northrop, inaugurated a movement which is improving the surroundings of schools in the rural districts almost beyond recognition, and in West Virginia the commendable efforts of the Department of Public Instruction, under the direction of Hon. B. L. Butcher, have resulted in similar improvements. The work of Dr. John B. Peaslee, City Superintendent of Cincinnati, in the same direction, has also been especially successful."

71. Now that Arbor Day in spring is one of the school institutions of the Province, it is desirable that the school grounds, and the outside strip in front of the school house and on the street, or road side, should be judiciously planted. Care should be taken to select the most suitable trees and shrubs for that purpose, considering the nature of the soil and the size of the school lot, etc. Flowers, too, should be provided for the beds in front of the buildings, and, if practicable, at the sides of the walks leading to the school entrances.

72. Mr. R. W. Phipps, who is an authority on Forestry in Ontario, has furnished the Minister of Education with the following list and explanatory information (which I have modified and condensed) on this subject :—

"1. The trees which experience proves to be best adapted to our Canadian climate are divided into several classes. First, the deciduous trees, which are easily grown that is to say, they have fibrous roots, rendering them easy to transplant. The young saplings, as they stand in the undergrowth of the forest, will be found with sufficient roots, if care be taken, to transplant well. The term deciduous is applied to all trees not evergreen.

"MAPLES.—Native Hard Maple (acer saccharinum); Scarlet or Soft Maple (acer rubrum); Silver Leaf Maple (acer dasycarpum); Norway Maple (acer platanoides); Ash Leaved Maple (acer negundo); [aceroides negundo of Dr. F. B. Hough, see paragraph No. 73.]

"ELMS.—American or White Elm (ulmus Americana); Cork Barked or Winged Elm (ulmus inflata); Scotch or Wych Elm (ulmus montana). (See paragraph No. 73.)

"LINDENS.—European Linden (tilea Europœa); Basswood (tilea Americana).

"ASH.—Native, white (fraxinus Americana); European Ash (fraxinus Europœa).

"CHESTNUTS.—Horse Chestnut (æsculus hippocastaneum); Sweet Chestnut (castanea Americana).

"MOUNTAIN ASH—Sorbus.

"2. The following native trees are also well adapted for transplanting, but they cannot be handled like the former, owing to their having but few roots. There are two ways of treating them—one, to plant the nuts where the tree is to grow, the other to transplant them several times when young. This gives them a mass of roots of far more certain growth for planting in their ultimate position.

"HARDWOOD TREES, such as Hickory (carya); Oaks (quercus); Beech (fagus); Walnut (juglans).

"3. The time for planting all of the above is in spring, from the time the frost leaves the ground, till May 15th. The season, however, can be prolonged to the 15th June, by observing to cut back the tops of the trees. In the fall the time of planting may be from the 20th of October till the ground is frozen too hard for digging. When planting them care should be taken to strip the leaves off, as the sap remaining in the trees soon evaporates through the leaves, causing them to shrivel up and so destroy their chance of growth.

"4. The next class peculiarly suited for transplanting is the evergreen. Those of the spruce and cedar variety are grown more easily than pines or junipers, as they have a greater quantity of good roots. This class comprises the White or Native Spruce (abies alba), Norway Spruce (abies excelsa), Balsam Spruce or Fir Proper (tsuga balsamifera), Hemlock (abies Canadensis), White Cedar (thuja occidentalis). The spruce

CHAP. VIII.   PLANTING THE SCHOOL GROUNDS.   41

and cedar family will grow in damper situations than will the pines, but all succeed better in fairly drained soil.

"5. The next variety of evergreen is the pine. Unless transplanted several times when young, these do not throw out many roots, and those thrown out are fine, long and easily disbarked, unless great care be taken in removing them from the soil. The most suitable varieties are :--

"PINES.—White Pine (pinus strobus); Weymouth Pine (pinus cembra); Norway Pine (pinus rubra); Austrian Pine (pinus Austriacea); Scotch Pine (pinus sylvestris).

'The planting season for all the above evergreens is from May 15th to June 15th, or just as the buds are commencing to burst.

"6. The last which need be noted is the larch.

"LARCHES.—European Larch (larix Europæa); Native Larch, Tamarac (larix Americana).

"This tree may be termed a deciduous evergreen, and succeeds best when planted late in the fall, or the first thing in spring. It commences to grow with the first warm rays of the sun, but is uncertain unless great care is taken to keep it damp. This advice is meant in case of large trees, such as those five to seven feet high. Small trees are grown more easily.

"7. With respect to soil, all trees thrive best in well-drained soil, varying from a sandy loam to a clay soil, not of too stiff a nature. A clay loam suits them all.

"8. If chestnut trees be planted in spring, the heads or leaves should not be cut off, as this tree makes all its growth in the first few growing days and is then stationary for the season. The branches may, if necessary, be thinned.

"9. When trees are finally planted, care should be taken to mulch around them with old manure, leaves, spent hops, straw, if it can be kept in place—stones laid on it do this—or other substance not injurious to growth, but never, for example, with pine sawdust or tanbark. Some cultivators prefer keeping the ground stirred to mulching.

"10. When transplanting evergreens, the roots should never be exposed to air or light—especially sun heat—more than can be helped. The root is resinous; if the resin hardens, the process of growth in future will be rendered impossible."

73. Dr. F. B. Hough, Chief of the Forestry Division of the United States Department of Agriculture, in a letter (on the planting of trees in school grounds) to Hon. John Eaton, Commissioner of Education, written in 1883, adds :—

1. "Of all the native trees of the Northern States, the American elm (ulmus Americana) is perhaps least liable to accident from a bruise upon the bark; and there are few, if any, that should be more generally preferred. It carries its shade high above the level of our windows; it is seldom broken or thrown down by the winds; it lives to a great age and grows to a large size, and it presents a majestic and graceful outline as agreeable to the view as its spreading canopy is refreshing in its shade. The red or slippery elm might be liable to be peeled by unruly boys, for its inner bark, and should for this reason be planted only upon private grounds.

2. "The maples are justly prized as shade trees, and the sugar maple (acer saccharinum) may, perhaps, be placed first on the list, as affording a dense shade and a graceful oval outline. . . . All of the maples are conspicuous in the declining year from the bright colouring of their autumnal foliage. The box elder, or ash-leaved maple (negundo

aceroides), a nearly allied species, is a favourite shade tree in the Western States, and grows well in the middle latitudes of the Atlantic States."

74. The shrubs suggested in the United States book on School Architecture are the Missouri currant, Barberry, Weigelia, Cornel, Laurel, Lilac, Roses (white, yellow, and red), Viburnum or Guelder rose, California privet, Forsythia, Spiræa, Tartarean honeysuckle, Dogwood, Deutzia. To these I add the following, which will grow freely in any part of Ontario, viz. :—Syringa, Yellow flowering currant, Hydrangea, Snowberry, Ashberry, etc. Of climbing shrubs I may mention the Virginia Creeper, Clematis, Bignonia radicans Birthwort, Roses, etc.

75. The Wisconsin State Superintendent of Schools adds :—

"1. Damp spots may be improved by covering them with clusters of the beautiful pyrus japonica, and porches may be ornamented by climbing vines, such as ivy (English, German, or the small leaved varieties), woodbine or wistaria, roses and honeysuckles [Virginia creeper, trumpet flower, clematis, etc.]: and if any one will take the trouble to sow the seeds in spring, the red and white cypress vines, the fragrant jessamine, morning glories, and the purple and white Japanese clematis, may be added.

"2. It is best to plant several varieties of shrubs together in clumps. The dark evergreens or the holly and laurel then set off the brighter kinds, and the mutual protection which they afford each other against the winds helps the growth of all."

76. Dr. F. B. Hough, Chief of the Forestry division of the United States Department of Agriculture, in his letter, quoted above, makes the following useful suggestions :—

"1. To secure success trees should be selected from nursery plantations or from those that have sprung up in open places, such as the seedling trees along fences, so that that there may be an abundance of the small fibrous roots. Without this precaution they will be very liable to fail. It should be further borne in mind, that if the roots are much exposed to the sun or to a cold or drying wind their vitality may be soon lost. Great care should be taken, if they are brought from an adjoining place and planted immediately, to retain as much soil among them as possible, and to prefer a damp and cloudy day. By placing the roots of the trees as soon as they are drawn from the ground upon a coarse strong sheet of canvas, and binding this around them, this object may be best secured. Straw or moss, a little dampened, will serve this purpose very well, and sometimes the trees may be set in a box or barrel with some of the better soil in which they grew, for their removal. Sometimes trees can be removed in winter with great advantage by digging a trench around them in the fall and allowing the earth to freeze, so that a disk, including the tree and its roots, may be removed entire. . . . The ends of broken roots should be cut off smooth before the tree is planted.

"2. The holes for the trees should be always made before the trees are brought on the ground. They should be somewhat larger and deeper than those needed in common planting on private lands, because it is desirable to give the trees the best possible opportunity at the start. The surface soil being generally the best, should be thrown up on one side, and the poorer soil from below on the other. In filling in, the better soil should be returned first, so as to be nearer the roots. In hard clayey soils great advantage is gained by digging the holes in the fall, so that the earth may be exposed to the weather through the winter. The holes might be loosely covered with boards when necessary. If the soil be somewhat sterile, a waggon-load of rich loam, compost, or wood's earth, placed below and around the roots, would be the cheapest means for insuring success. In applying manures care should be taken that they be placed below and near, but not in contact with the roots. In setting the tree it should be placed a trifle deeper than it stood before, the roots should be spread out so that none are doubled, and fine rich soil should be carefully sifted in among them so as to fill every space. Sometimes the roots are dipped in a tub containing a thin mud of rich soil before they are set. In any event, unless the soil is evidently damp enough, the trees should be well watered as soon as they are planted, and this process in dry seasons should be repeated from time to time through the first and second years."

77. The Wisconsin State Superintendent further adds:—

"1. The constant care for these shrubs and trees and their unrivalled beauty help to educate the children; their shade is very grateful in the summer; they cool the atmosphere in the hot days by condensing moisture upon their leaves at night, and by evaporating vast amounts of it through their leaves in the day time; they absorb or destroy the poisonous gases and the noxious exhalations often found about the school buildings; and they produce a constant motion in the atmosphere, tending toward slight and healthful breezes.

"2. No shrub or tree should be planted . . . near the school building, where it will interfere with the light admitted through the windows."

78. The United States work on School Architecture, referring to this latter point, says:—

"The good effect of trees is reversed by allowing them to stand too near a building. While they may actually be used to dry up a marshy spot, by the great quantity of water which they take up through their roots and disperse by means of their leaves into the air, these same roots, near a cellar wall, will keep it damp as would the vicinity of a great wet sponge; and the shade of their branches, if allowed to fall on the school house, not only deprives it of so much wholesome sunshine, but the moving shadows on the windows or curtains cause a flickering of the light which is distressing and injurious to the eyes."

79. As to the flower beds suggested, the variety of annuals is so numerous that it is not necessary here to name any. A writer, already quoted, says:—

"A judicious selection of seeds, supplemented by slips from private gardens and young shoots transplanted from the woods, will cost almost nothing, while the civilizing influence of their beauty upon the children's minds, together with the pride and interest which their gardening operations will awaken, should not be undervalued."

80. Speaking of the value and usefulness of collections of native woods made by pupils of a school, Dr. F. B. Hough, before quoted, makes the following practical suggestions as to how and why such collections should be made:—

"There is no school house in the country, whether in city or village or rural district, which might not have at slight expense an interesting collection of the native woods of the vicinity. These **specimens** should **be prepared** by having one or more faces planed and polished or **varnished** to show the grain of **the** wood when worked to best advantage, and another face **simply** planed and **left in its** natural colour. There should be some portion of **the bark, and** it would be **still better if** there were shown in connection with the wood **dried specimens** of the **leaves and** blossoms, the fruit, and the resinous or other products. Such collections made up by the scholars, and correctly labelled, under the care of the teachers, would become object lessons of first importance as an agency for instruction. They would afford the most profitable kind of employment for the leisure hours, and might awaken a love of close observation and a thirst for further knowledge that would ripen into the best of fruits."

CHAPTER IX.

FENCE AND SCHOOL ENTRANCES.

"3. *The school grounds should be . . . enclosed by a substantial fence.*"—*Regulations, 1885.*

81. **Every school** lot should be substantially fenced in. Local taste will determine the kind of fence,—whether paling, board or picket, etc. A **rustic fence, if** well put together, is very neat and inexpensive. It may **be of** red cedar or other durable poles, with the bark on, consisting of posts **with top** and bottom rails well secured together and the intervals filled with pieces **of** random lengths nailed in any direction, the only care needed being to keep the network so formed uniformly open, not thick **in one part** and thin in another.

Fig. 14.—Sample of Fence **Paling** and Gate.

82. If a paling or picket fence be **preferred**, the following suggestions by the Wisconsin State School Superintendent are useful and valuable:—

"The lower portion of its posts, before buried **in the** ground, should be dipped in hot coal tar, which aids in preserving the wood a **much longer time.** Four well-planed boards of pine,—the bottom one eight or ten inches wide, and the rest each six inches, should be nailed, at the proper spaces from each other, on the posts set in the ground; and then a pine board,—four or five inches wide, fastened flat to the top of the post, cut even with, or slightly inclined toward, the highest board on the side. The fence should be painted in an agreeable and lasting color.* The gates should be strongly built, and so hung that they will shut themselves [and open either way]. An entrance way for the school, in the style here illustrated [or a turn-stile], will be found very convenient. It effectually excludes cattle from the enclosure; while it permits children and even adults to pass through with no difficulty. The opening in the fence next to the street should be four feet wide, and the passage inside two feet."

Separate Entrances to the School For Boys and Girls.

"12. *There should be separate entrances with covered porches and suitable cloak rooms for boys and girls.*"—*Regulations, 1885.*

83. There should be two separate entrances to every school house—one for boys and the other for girls.† This provision is now almost universal; and all the new and approved school houses have two entrances. Experience and the fitness of things, as well as the discipline and *morale* of the school, require these entrances to be separate. The United States book on School Architecture says:—

"1. The entrances, which must be separate for the two sexes, should be so planned that both boys and girls may be under the eye of the teacher in entering and leaving the room. They may be in the wall behind him, a very common position, but are better either in the side or opposite end walls, so that without turning his head, his glance may follow them through the vestibules until they are out of the building. This plan will prevent the silly tricks which children carry on in the vestibules sheltered from the teacher's observation, to the amusement of their fellows but to the detriment of discipline. The best arrangement will be to put one entrance door in the side wall, near the teacher's end of the room, and the other in the opposite end wall.

"2. The side door may be appropriated to the boys, who will thus be nearer the teacher and more under his control in entering and departing, and the end door, which will be behind the pupils, to the girls.

"3. The room being lighted alike on both sides, the pupils may sit facing either the east or west, but there are many advantages in arranging them to face the west. By this disposition the girls' entrance is brought on the sunniest and most sheltered part of the building, as it should be, and in interior planning, the stove or furnace, which must be at the north west corner of the room, comes in front of the pupils, where it finds the largest space and where its heat is diffused with the greatest comfort to all.

"4. Aspect must also be considered in regard to the entrances, which, in a word, should always face the south. A south entrance gives a breathing place for the children in rainy or blustering weather as they approach or leave the building, and protection to the interior from the March north-westers or easterly rain storms, which will blow in

---
* With coarse sand mixed with last coat of paint.
† See Official Regulation on this subject, preceding paragraph No. 81, page 44. See also block plan, Fig. 15, on page 48.

at an outside door exposed to them with such force as to make themselves felt through the whole school room whenever the door is opened; it gives dry and clean approaches to the building after snow storms, in place of impassable drifts; and last, but not least, shelter for those too punctual scholars who are sure to arrive before the building is open in the morning.

"5. So important has experience shown the southerly aspect for entrances to be that to this necessity is perhaps due the fashion of east and west lighting for the school room proper. . . .

"6. There may be situations where a south exposure is impracticable for one or both entrances. In such a case, much may be done by contriving porches, which, although entered from the east or west, or even from the north, can have wide windows toward the south, and angles or screens which may shelter the early arrivals from the cold winds."

84. The State School Superintendent of Wisconsin also gives a good reason for separate entrances to the school. He says:—

"It tends to prevent crowding and disorder of the pupils before reaching, or on leaving, the school rooms, and removes the temptation for boys and girls to remain in the entries engaged in conversation."

The Vestibules and Cloak Rooms, or Wardrobes.

85. The author of the United States Book on School Architecture, speaking of vestibules and wardrobes, says:—

"1. A good rule for vestibules is that the outside doors shall be placed at an angle with those opening from the vestibules into the school room. This will cut off the direct impulse of the wind and exclude draughts with ten times the effectiveness of outside and vestibule doors in parallel walls. They should be light and sufficiently spacious to give the crowd which pours out of the school room doors at recess a little breathing space before they are pushed into the open air.*

"2. Attached to each vestibule should be a . . . wardrobe. These may open directly from the school room. . . . but the smell of wet clothes in rainy weather . . . is penetrating and disagreeable, and a better disposition is to open the wardrobes from the vestibules, these being at the same time so arranged that the teacher can observe everything that goes on in either of them.†

---

* In constructing the entrances to a school house it should be remembered that the Canadian law requires that the doors should be made to open outwards.

Care should also be taken to make the staircases and passages of the school house of more than one story as wide as possible, so as to facilitate the egress of the pupils in case of fire or panic. Pupils should also be drilled to leave the school house in the shortest possible time so as to prevent crushing in case of alarm. (See paragraph number 129, on fire drill, page 74.)

† Dr. D. T. Lincoln, in the Report for 1882, of the New York State Board of Health, says on this point:—" It is not proper to hang overclothes in the rooms where scholars sit. A closed wardrobe . . . . in the school room condenses the effluvia and concentrates the effect of packing a quantity of most reeking [garments]. The chance of diffusing infection is increased by such contact. [The wardrobe] should be large enough [so that the] clothes should hang without overlapping each other. It should have good light and free circulation of air, and be well warmed."

"3. Besides the wardrobes, each vestibule should be furnished with washbowls and roller towels. . . . .* All that is needful is a common cistern pump in each vestibule [to the rainwater tank], with a lead or enamelled iron suction pipe to the well, and an earthenware or tinned copper basin, or sink if preferred, with a waste pipe to a dry well outside. This will cost [such] a trifle [that] at 6 per cent. interest, ... the cost of keeping a school of 50 pupils clean [would not exceed 10] cents each a year. . . .

"4. The pumps may be had with a pin hole in the valve, so that the water cannot stand long enough in them to freeze, and traps in the waste pipe may be dispensed with as unnecessary, so that there will be no other part of the apparatus to be injured by frost."

86. Leading up to the entrances, flower beds might (as provided by the regulations relating to Arbor Day) be placed with advantage, thus adding beauty, as well as sources of pleasure and instruction to the teachings of the school. (See block plan, Fig. 15, in next chapter.)

CHAPTER X.

PLAN OF THE SCHOOL GROUNDS.

"5. *The area of a school site should not be less than half an acre in extent, and if t school population of the section exceeds seventy-five, the area should be one acre.*"—*Regulations, 1885.*

"9. *The school house should be placed at least thirty feet from the public highway.*"—*Ibid.*

87. It is only in a general way that suggestions in regard to the arrangements and plans of the school grounds can be of practical value. The school authorities in each locality must determine such questions for themselves.

88. As a rule the entrances to the school, or at least the front of the building, should face the south, or the east—never the north, unless it be a matter of necessity.† The well, outbuildings, shade trees, flower beds, etc., should be placed, as nearly as possible, in the positions indicated in block plan, fig. 15, and in the chapters devoted to these special subjects. In placing the school house, so as to admit the light only from the north or east, it will be necessary to consider the whole matter well before erecting the house. With a view to give practical effect to what I have hitherto said on this subject, I insert the following block plan on the next page, by way of suggestion and illustration.

---

* See paragraph No. 57 on Lavatories, page 32.
† See, also, in this connection the chapter (XIV.) on Lighting and Windows.

48 PLAN OF SCHOOL GROUNDS. CHAP. X.

89. The following plan may be modified according to circumstances, but the main features of it should be retained, especially in regard to the privies, play grounds and play sheds.

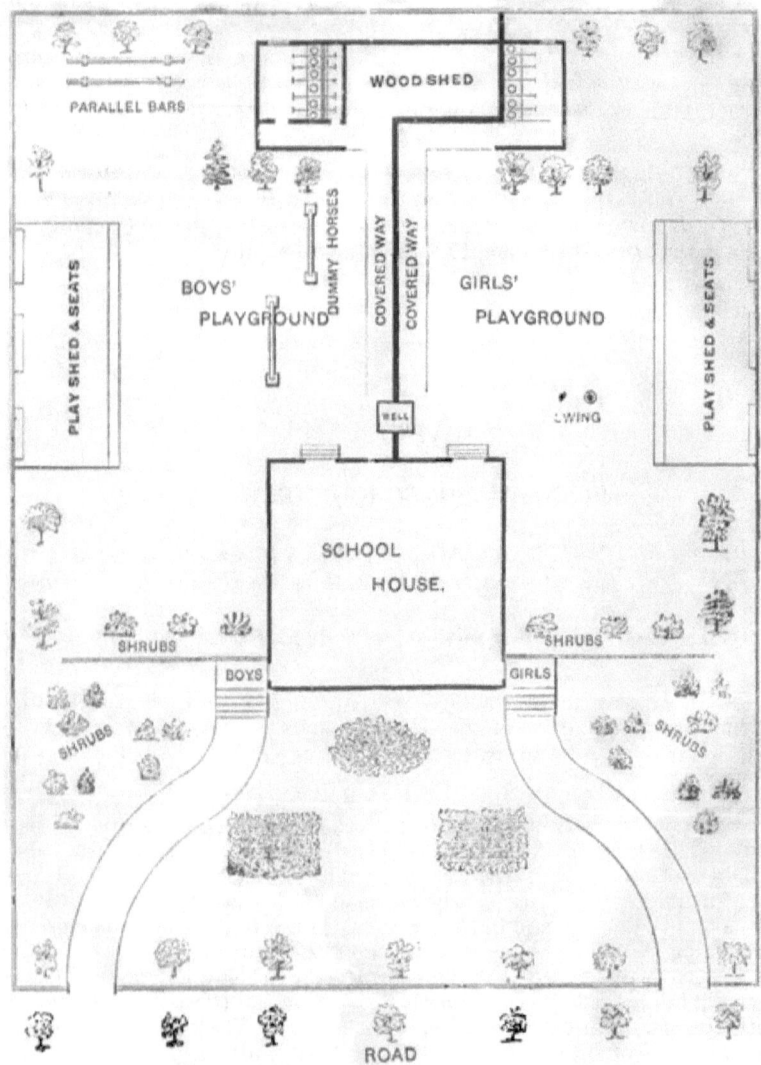

FIG. 15.—BLOCK PLAN OF SCHOOL GROUNDS.

CHAP. X.   PLAN OF SCHOOL GROUNDS.   49

90. The New Brunswick Board of Education have suggested a plan of school grounds which I give in the following diagram (fig. 16) as an alternative to my own. It differs from the foregoing, but not in very import-

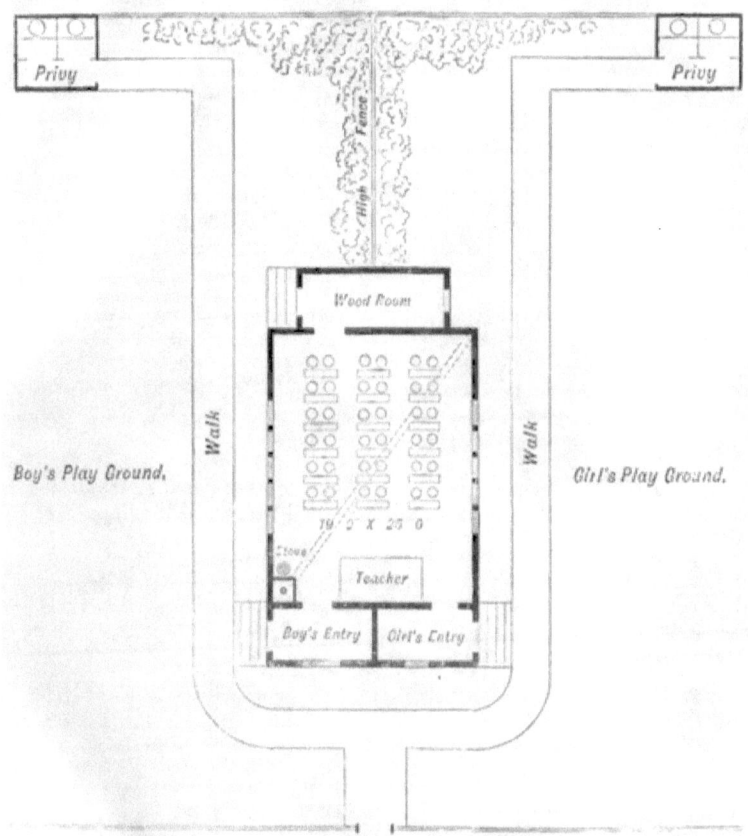

FIG. 16.—BLOCK PLAN OF SCHOOL GROUNDS.

ant particulars. It, however, lacks the convenience of play sheds for the children, as well as a separate entrance for girls from the road and from their play grounds in the rear. Trees, flowers and shrubs should be added if the plan be adopted.

CHAPTER XI.

THE CONSTRUCTION OF SCHOOL HOUSES.

91. As a preliminary to the consideration of the important subject of school house construction, I desire to refer to the proceedings on this subject which took place at the International Educational Congress held in Brussels in August, 1880. At that Congress, this subject, in its hygienic aspect, received the greatest attention.

92. Dr. W. T. Harris, a distinguished educationist, now of Concord, Massachusetts, was deputed by the American National Educational Association to attend this Congress and report the results. In his report of the Congress to the Association in 1881, he says:—

"Fifteen specialists of different countries (Belgium, France, Great Britain, Hungary, Holland, Russia and Switzerland), sent in reports on six questions proposed, and these are very complete, and bearing the traces of very thorough study. Seven reports and six supplementary ones were sent in by scientific men of different nationalities. . . . The assembly devoted much time to the principal hygienic conditions to be observed in the construction of school buildings.

93. Dr. Harris then gives the result of these deliberations in the following condensed form, which I have still further abbreviated, viz.:

"1. The lighting of day class-rooms (the subject of three reports) was considered at length, and the following resolution adopted : ' Class-rooms should be lighted during the day by windows, on one side only, and to the left of the pupils. They should be so arranged that all the seats would be fully and equally lighted, the question of ventilation being considered apart from that of lighting.'

"2. The question of the proper cubic contents of air was settled by the following resolution : 'The length of a class-room, the maximum number should be 9.60 metres, the width 6.60 metres to 8 metres'—(or thirty-one by twenty-one to twenty-six feet.)

"3. The section . . . was unanimous in deciding in favor of single desks, such as are in use in many schools on the continent.

"4. . . . The section adopted a resolution in favor of extending medical inspection to the schools. . . . The section also resolved :—

"5. That the Belgian Government should take the initiative in establishing throughout the kingdom—after the example set by Brussels—hygienic statistics in schools, that will show the influence of schools on the health of children."

94. In addition to these valuable suggestions, I quote others from an experienced American authority—Hon. John D. Philbrick, LL.D At the request of Hon. John Eaton, United States Commissioner of Education, he prepared an elaborate report on the "school systems in the cities of the United States," which was published by the Bureau of Edu-

cation this year (1885), as one of the "**circulars** of information."* At the conclusion of his report, Dr. Philbrick sums up his criticisms on the existing school buildings (which he describes) in a **series** of suggestions which are so valuable and recent that I quote them at length. He says, speaking of the

"REQUIREMENTS OF A MODEL SCHOOL ROOM.

(1) "*Shape.*—It should be oblong, the width being to the length about as three to four, with the teacher's platform at one end.

(2) "*Size.*—For a primary . . . school with a register of 54 pupils and attendance of about 50, the room should be 33 feet long by 25 wide and 13 feet high, which gives practically **upwards of 200 cubic** feet and $16\frac{1}{2}$ square feet of floor space to each pupil.

(3) "*Lighting.*—From **windows on the left** of the pupils as they sit, the tops being square and not more than six inches from the ceiling, the bottom being at least three and a half feet from the floor, equally spaced, not grouped, with transome sashes hung at the case, above the sliding sashes. A window or two, in addition, at the back is admissible. The size of the windows on **the side, taken** collectively, should be equal at least to one-sixth of the **floor** space. The highest authorities in school hygiene require 300 or 350 square inches of glass for each pupil.†

(4) "*Doors.*—On the side opposite the windows, two doors with transome windows above, hung at the base, and between these transome windows, and on the same line, two more windows of the same kind and hung in the same manner.

(5) "*Walls.*—The walls should be slightly tinted, but not the ceiling.

(6) "*Blackboard.*—A blackboard may be between the doors, but a sliding blackboard, back of the teacher's platform, or a portable one on the platform, in accordance with the German idea, would perhaps be better than the profusion of wall blackboard now in vogue among us.

(7) "*Seating.*—The main rule to be observed in the placing of the seats is to carry them as far as possible from the opposite side; the aim being to make the arrangement such that the distance of **the outer row of desks from the windows shall not exceed** once and a half the height of the top of the window from the floor.

---

* In referring to Dr. **Philbrick's** qualification for this work, Hon. John Eaton says :—"**John D. Philbrick,** LL.D., became Superintendent of the **Boston** school in January, 1857, having previously been a teacher in these schools, Principal of **the** Connecticut Normal School, and Superintendent of public instruction **for that** State. It is acknowledged the world over, that to him is largely and specially due the **excellence of the** Boston schools. A thorough man of affairs, accurate and broad in his scholarship, . . . he not only **watched and guided the** Boston schools that grew under his hands for twenty years, **but, by travels and studies** in different parts of this country, **and** during two visits to Europe, . . . he had the rarest opportunities for extensive personal observation elsewhere in **school** matters, and for philosophical deductions therefrom. . . . He had official duties in connection with the exhibition at Vienna, and the special organization, **care** and management of the **American** Exhibition **of** Education at Paris in 1878."

† In another part **of his** report, quoted in Chapter XVII., Dr. Philbrick lays stress on the great desirability of **so** placing the school house **that** its angles shall **be in the** same direction as are the four cardinal points of the compass. (See Chapter XVII.)

(8) *Wardrobes, or Clothes Rooms.*—There are three kinds of [wardrobes, viz.] : (1) One room [set apart] for the whole school or several classes ; (2) a room attached to each school room ; (3) arrangements within each school room, either wardrobes, or racks, or pegs on the wall. The second kind is most prevalent and is thought by some to be indispensable ; it has important advantages, but its use by both sexes, promiscuously, is decidedly objectionable. . . . [The third kind is very undesirable, for the reasons given in note † to paragraph, number 85 page 46.]

95. No one can over-estimate the great practical value of these expressions of opinion on the subject under consideration, from authorities so distinguished as the Brussels Congress of Educationists, and the American school report of Dr. Philbrick. They embody the latest and most carefully considered judgments of some of the leading educators and professional experts in Europe and America, on school house construction. As such, they deserve candid and careful consideration on the part of those who are by law entrusted with the duty of providing school house accommodation for the youth of our country.

96. It may be urged that in "the good old days," and in the early times in this country, no one ever thought of prescribing rules on subjects of this kind, or even of making any suggestions on such matters. True. But the consequence was, that we then unwittingly sacrificed many youthful lives, and would persistently have continued to do so, had not medical experience and remonstrance, by calling attention to the subject, arrested the evil. At all events, we have now the fullest and most satisfactory information on the subject, gathered from all quarters, and that too of unquestionable authority. We would then be acting a most cruel and unjust part to the children of this country were we not cheerfully to avail ourselves of the wise counsels and extensive experience of those who are not only competent to advise us in these matters, but who give us such facts and data on the subject, as should convince any reasonable man that what is suggested is the right and wise thing to do, so as to conserve the precious lives of the children committed to our care and instruction.

Details of School Building Construction.*

97. It is not necessary to go much into detail in regard to the building of a School House, but there are certain important matters in connection with it which merit careful attention. They relate (1) to the foundation ; (2) the walls ; (3) the floors ; (4) internal fittings, such as wainscoting, blackboards, etc. The matter of ventilation, windows, seating and other details will be referred to in a subsequent chapter.

1. *The foundation.* Whether the building be a frame, brick, or stone one, great care should be taken to make the foundation secure, and

---

* For obvious reasons I have not gone into the minutiæ of building in this chapter. What I have said on the matter referred to in the text is designed to aid rural trustees by hint and suggestion in framing their contracts or agreements with builders, and in preparing specifications.

CHAP. XI.   DETAILS OF SCHOOL BUILDING CONSTRUCTION.   53

especially to see that it is thoroughly drained. Even if posts alone be used to support a frame structure, the same care as to drainage is necessary, so as to prevent dampness and its consequent evils.

98. In this connection, and in regard to the preliminary mechanical details, I give the following valuable suggestions, based upon the experience and judgment of the skilled architect who has prepared the United States work on School Architecture. He thus points out what should be done so as to secure a good foundation, and also how the work itself should be performed

(a) "The site having been carefully selected and drained as before described, the cellar may be excavated to a uniform depth of about 3 feet below the original surface of the ground. The sod, if good, should be stripped off and utilized at once in improving the remoter portions of the lot. The loam should be piled separately, to be put subsequently on top of the grading. The gravel or earth will be disposed of as the nature of the ground may require, but on a reasonably level spot all the excavated material will generally be used in raising the ground to a gentle slope around the building; not a steep bank, but a grade of one in ten or so. The trenches for the foundation walls should be dug 2 feet below the cellar bottom and 18 inches of dry stone filled in and rammed down before starting the walls; the excavation should be made 8 inches larger than the wall, as before described, and the wall carried up with smooth outside face to the height set for the under side of the first floor. This will vary according to circumstances. If the building is to be warmed by a furnace, the height of the basement should be about 8 feet. Not only is anything less than this insufficient to give head room under the hot-air pipes, but the heating is much more certain where the basement is high enough to allow a good pitch to the hot-air pipes. If there is no furnace, 6½ feet clear will give sufficient head room. . . The thickness of the foundation depends upon the material and upon the thickness of the wall above. Where it can be procured, rubble stone, of granite, slate, greenstone, trap, or any of the harder rocks, makes a perfectly satisfactory foundation for a building of the kind proposed, being comparatively impervious, and therefore little liable to soak up ground moisture, to give it out again from the inner surface; while, for the same reason, the ground does not freeze to the outside in winter, gradually tearing to pieces a wall built of them, as it does a brick or soft stone foundation in cold climates. If the wall above is of rubble it will be usually 16 inches thick, and the foundation must be from 20 to 24 inches thick, according to the character of the stone, rounded bowlders demanding greater thickness than the flat pieces of slate. A hollow brick wall above will be from 12 to 16 inches thick, and a 20-inch rubble or 16-inch brick foundation will suffice. A frame building, if there is a cellar under it, should have a rubble wall 18 to 20 inches thick, according to the character of the stone, or a 12-inch brick wall will do if it is protected against the pressure of earth from outside and from the disintegrating action of frost in clayey and clinging soils by a good thick envelope of clean gravel. A solid 8-inch brick wall above will need a similar foundation. If no cellar is required, the trench wall for the foundation should still be 18 inches thick, if of stone, or 12 inches, if of brick. Nothing less than these will long withstand the winter frosts. . .

(b) [As] "frame buildings [which have no cellars for hot-air furnaces] are very generally built on piers or posts. . . . With strong sills and good piers this is a durable and economical construction. [In this case the sills should be raised] well above the ground. If earth is graded up against the sills they will inevitably rot in [time. The space, therefore, between the sills and the ground might] be filled in with sawed sheeting, [such as shown in this illustration (fig. 17). Any other pattern can be chosen].

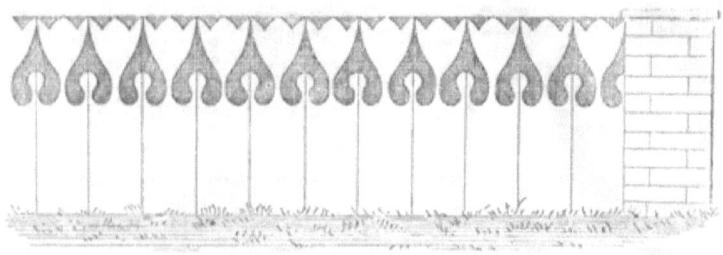

FIG. 17.—SAWED SHEETING FOR FOUNDATION COURSE.

(c) "The piers of a frame building without cellarage should be very substantial, 18 inches square, if of rubble stone, or 12 by 12, if of brick. The 8 by 12 or 8 by 8 brick piers commonly used begin to bend in a few years. Wooden posts may with advantage and economy in many cases be made of spruce lumber [soaked in tar or other timber preservative] . . .

(d) "Whatever kind of basement is adopted, ample openings for ventilation should be provided. It is true that a well aired cellar, unless there is a furnace in it, makes it necessary to plaster the cellar ceiling or to lay the upper floors double, to prevent them from being intolerably cold in winter; but this is only part of the price which must be paid for a wholesome and enduring structure."

2. *The Walls* above the basement will be of brick, stone, or wood, according to circumstances.

"Solid brick walls of the required height may be 12 or even 8 inches thick, and must be furred with wooden strips 1 by 2 inches, nailed to the inside, and these strips lathed and plastered, the air spaces thus formed between the plastering and the inner surface of the wall being necessary to keep external dampness from penetrating into the room. Stone walls must be at least 16 inches thick, and the roughness of their inner surface rendering it impossible to nail furring strips to them, independent studding must be set up inside, precisely as in the case of a frame building, and this lathed and plastered."

99. As these furred walls are dangerous, when fire occurs, in conveying sparks and flame from the basement to the roof, the writer very properly says that—

(a) "The only effectual remedy for these evils lies in the use of hollow walls, of brick throughout or with stone facing, as may be preferred, and such walls are by far the best to inclose school rooms.

(b) "Such a wall, of the height proposed, should be 16 inches thick, the air space being 4 inches, the outer wall 8, and lining wall 4 inches, and tied by continuous "withs" at intervals of about two feet. Each "width" is to be built with headers bonded alternately into the outer and inner walls. The corners should be built solid. (See Fig. 28.)

CHAP. XI.   DETAILS OF SCHOOL BUILDING CONSTRUCTION.   55

(c) "The outer wall should be of the hardest bricks, the semi-vitrification of the surface being very necessary to prevent the conduction of water from the outside into the lining wall.

(d) "The inside of the air space should be made reasonably smooth, leaving holes at the bottom to facilitate cleaning out, and at the completion of the wall all mortar and shavings, remnants, ... and other vestiges of the workmen's presence, should be cleared out and the holes built up. At the cornice the air space will be covered over and a level bed of mortar spread for bedding the plate. A small opening should be left at the bottom of each air space opening into the basement, and another at the top opening into the external air. By these a constant current of air will be maintained through the hollow. This is essential to the dryness of the wall.

(e) "It is best to build ⅝ or ¾ inch iron bolts into the solid work at the corners to secure the plate. These should be 2 feet long and have a washer 2 by 4 inches or so at the bottom, and must be so set that 4 or 4½ inches of the upper end will project above the top of the wall.

(f) "A screw thread is cut on it and corresponding holes are bored in the plate, so that when this is laid on, the ends of the bolts will appear above the upper surface, and washer and nuts are then applied and screwed down. By this means the roof is firmly held to the walls.

(g) "A simple cornice may be formed by projecting bricks,"—as in the following illustrations : (Figs. 18 and 19.)

FIG. 18.—CORNICE OF PROJECTING BRICKS AND SECTION, No. 1.

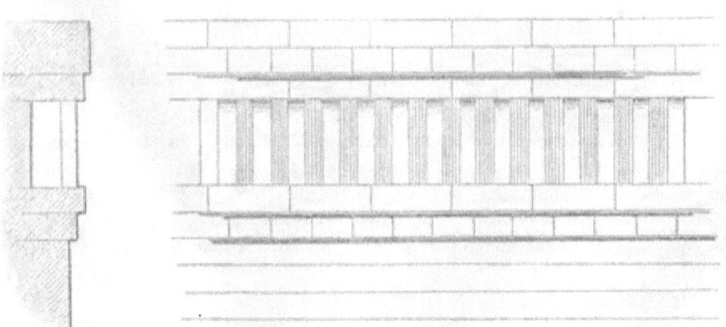

FIG. 19.—CORNICE OF PROJECTING BRICKS AND SECTION, No. 2.

(*h*) "In such buildings, ... a considerable expense is saved and a picturesque effect obtained outside, as well as great advantages for lighting and ventilation inside.

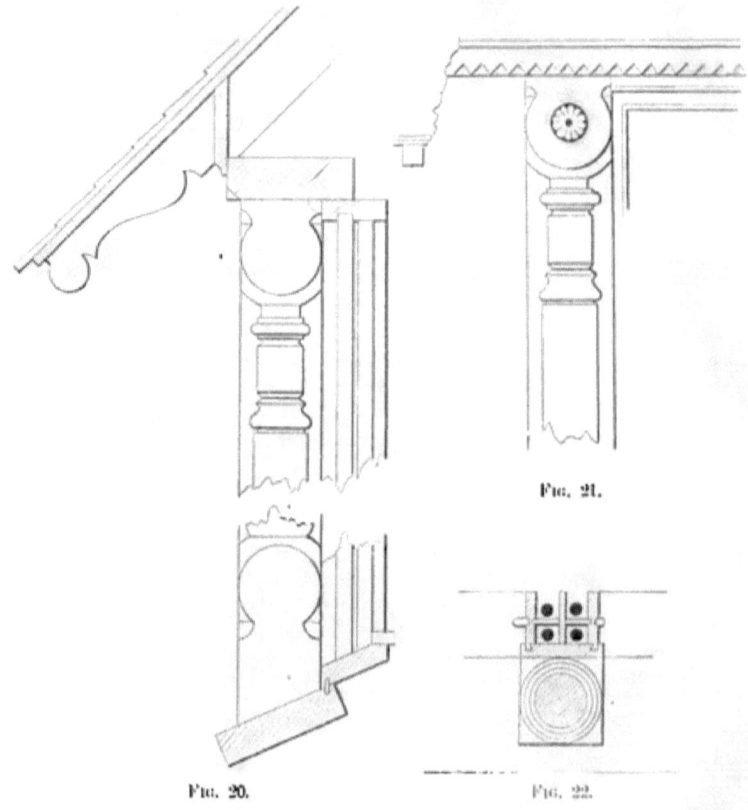

FIGS. 20, 21, 22.—WINDOW OPENINGS,—SECTIONS AND DETAILS.

by carrying [as shown in the illustrations, Figs. 20-22] the window openings up to the under side of the wall plate, without arch or lintel.*

(*i*) A cornice of brick may be made, if desired (as shown in the following illustration, Fig. 23, and in Figs. 18 and 19), stopping at the window openings. The wall may be finished without any projection, and the edge of the plate may be moulded or cut either on the solid, or by planting on "mill mouldings;" or the square edge of the timber may be cut into a "dog-tooth" or other ornaments (as shown in figures 24-27).

---

* The Regulations (No. 14) require that the "windows (both sashes) should be adjusted by weights and pulleys and provided with blinds."

CHAP. XI.   DETAILS OF SCHOOL BUILDING CONSTRUCTION.   57

(j) "The ordinary bond for an 8-inch wall, which consists of a continuous row of headers every sixth or seventh course (as shown in Fig. 28), will give the wall the appearance of being barred with faint horizontal lines, 10 or 15 inches apart.

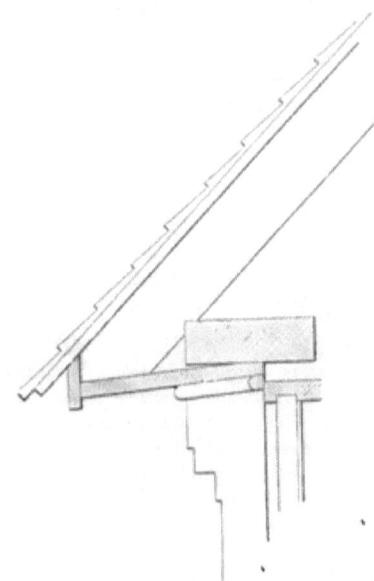

FIG. 23.—SECTION OF BRICK CORNICE.

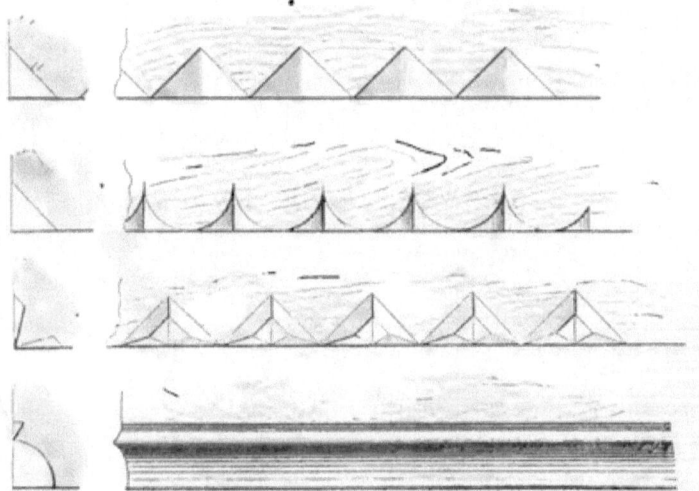

FIGS. 24-27.—PLATE MOULDINGS, DOG-TOOTH AND OTHER ORNAMENTS, WITH SECTIONS.

FIG. 28.—SYSTEM OF BRICK BONDINGS.

100. The following suggestions I have, for convenience, condensed:

3. *Floors.** The floor beams should be laid sixteen inches apart from centre to centre. It is a mistake often made to notch the sill for the beams and cut these with a projecting tenon two inches deep, or so, at the upper edge, so that when this is laid in the notch the top of the beams is flush with that of the sill. By this bad arrangement, not only do the beams hang down below the sill, so as to interfere with the foundation wall, to its and their detriment, but (as shown in figure 29), the tenon is very liable to split off, thus dangerously weakening the floor.

A much better way is not to mortice the sill at all, but to notch the beams to within four inches of the top, lay them in place and spike them through the side (as shown in figure 30). In this case the tenon will not split off, and the mortising of the sill—a great source of rot—is avoided.

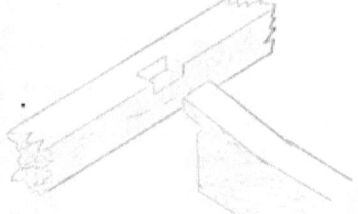

FIG. 29.—A NOTCHED SILL.

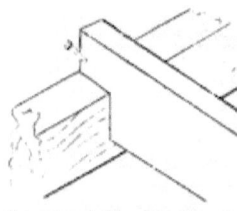

FIG. 30.—A NOTCHED BEAM.

101. *Wainscoting* should be pannelled (as shown in Fig. 31), or may be in any other pattern.

(*a*) The objection to sheeting is that the joints in it shrink unequally, even when half of them are not mere imitations, and the work soon begins to look ragged and cheap almost as soon as finished, especially in the hot school room, while the seams afford harbour for insects. Wainscoting will look well and give a finish to the room.

---

* Dr. Covernton, in an article on "Medical Inspection of Schools," published in the Report for 1883 of the Provincial Board of Health, says that "On the Continent, great exception is properly taken to pine floors, as they are quickly worn, the knots projecting, the wood around splintering, and becoming collectors of mud and dust. In a season of colds and influenza, the children cough and spit, the expectorations dry, and the infected dust spreads catarrh or it may be the germs of phthisis in the school-room. Flooring should, therefore, always be [of hard wood]."

CHAP. XI.   DETAILS OF SCHOOL BUILDING CONSTRUCTION.   59

Under the windows the **wainscot** should be **the whole** height from **floor to** window sill—four feet. For *very cheap* work, the panels **may be** ⅜ inch boards nailed to the wall, and **the** framing, or "**stiles**" also of ⅜ **inch pieces** neatly fitted and **nailed at** top.

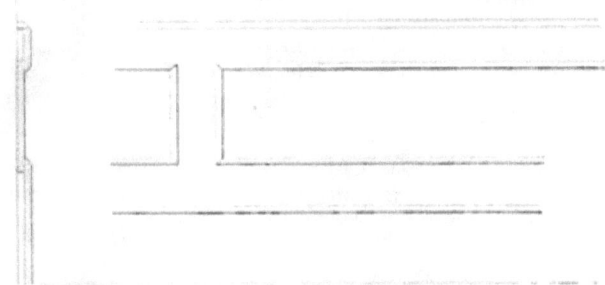

FIG. 31.—PANELLED **WAINSCOTING** AND SECTION.

(*b*) Wainscoting should be finished **with a bevel or** quarter round, **which on the side walls may form** a continuation of the stoolcap moulding of the **windows.** Under the blackboards **it is common to** finish with a moulding either shaped **out of the solid into a trough** on the top, or **supporting** a separate one, which may be simply a strip of **half-inch** board, inclined towards the blackboard (as in fig. 33). This is to catch **chalk** dust and hold **crayons** and **rubbers.**

(*c*) **Hallways** and vestibules **may** with advantage **also be** wainscoted in **the same simple** manner, **three or four** feet high. Door and **window** architraves [**should be**] **very** simple.

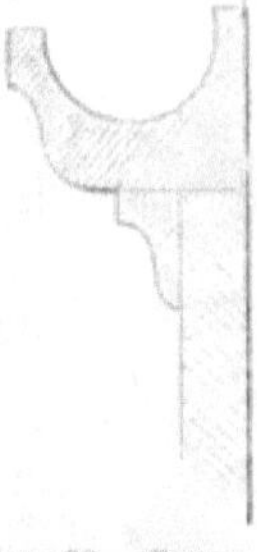

102. *Blackboards.* The Regulations (No. 22) direct that—

"**There should be one** blackboard at least four feet **wide, extending across** the whole room in rear of the teacher's desk, with its lower **edge not** more than two and a half feet **above the** floor or platform, and, when possible, there should be an additional blackboard on each side **of the room.** At the lower edge of each blackboard **there should be a** shelf or trough five inches wide for holding crayons and **brushes.**"*

FIG. 32.—CHALK TRAY MOULDING, NO. 1.

FIG. 33.—CHALK TRAY MOULDING, NO. 2.

---

* The following directions for making a blackboard [appended to the regulation] may be found useful:—

(*a*) **If the walls** are brick the plaster should be laid upon the brick and not upon the laths as elsewhere ; if frame, the part to be used for a blackboard should be lined with boards, and the laths for holding **the** plaster nailed firmly on the boards.

(*b*) The plaster **for** the blackboard should **be composed** largely of plaster of Paris.

(*c*) Before and **after having** received the **first coat of** color it should be thoroughly polished with fine sand paper.

(*d*) The coloring matter should be laid **on with a** wide, flat varnish brush.

(*e*) **The liquid coloring** should be made as follows:—Dissolve gum shellac in alcohol, four ounces **to the quart ; the** alcohol should be 95 **per cent.** strong ; the dissolving process will require **at least twelve hours.** Fine emery flour **with enough** chrome green or lampblack to give color,

103. These blackboards should properly be slabs of smooth slate, secured with iron bolts fastened to the brickwork. Or the blackboard space may be plastered with the ordinary coating of "liquid slating" which will make a much better blackboard than the usual lathing covered with soft lime plaster and lampblack or other expedient.* The blackboard should be finished with a small moulding at the top and also with a moulding, in the shape of a tray, as shown in the accompanying figures, 30 and 31. These trays should have a small grating of iron, or of wire at each end through which the chalk dust may be brushed.

104. *Brushes* for the blackboard can generally be obtained from those who supply school requisites. Any teacher, however, can readily make them by fastening a piece of sheepskin to a block of wood shaped like a shoe-brush. The sheepskin, with the woolly side out, can be tacked to the back of the brush. It can be used with or without a handle, as the teacher may prefer.

CHAPTER XII.

HEATING AND VENTILATION.

The General Principles of Ventilation.

105. Ventilation is a large and difficult subject. Much has been written upon it, and many theories held in regard to it. The principle is, after all, simple enough, and yet the great difficulty has been to apply this simple principle in an effective and practical way.

106. The principle and aim of ventilation are thus explained in the United States work on School Architecture:—

"Briefly, the aim of ventilation should be to maintain a steady supply of fresh air and withdrawal of foul at all parts of the room, removing the products of respiration and organic particles as fast as thrown off, and leaving no corner stagnant or unswept by the purifying current."

107. This writer goes on to point out the difference between natural and artificial ventilation. He says, and says truly :—

"1. Nothing can take the place of aeration by means of open windows. Artificial ventilation, though required for changing the air when the windows are necessarily closed, is insufficient, even under the best of circumstances, unless the room is from time to time thoroughly refreshed and purified by the sweep of the free winds through all its windows widely opened. Such an atmospheric washing should be secured three

---

should then be added until the mixture has the consistency of thin paint. It may then be applied, in long, even strokes, up and down, the liquid being kept constantly stirred.

* As to the position of the blackboards; see paragraph number 94 (6) and number 145 (7).

CHAP. XII. HEATING AND VENTILATION—WINDOW OPENINGS.   61

or four times daily in all weathers; at recess, particularly, it should be insisted on, banishing teachers and pupils from the room meanwhile, if necessary. They will more than make up in the brightness of the remaining hours for the time they may thus lose. Immediately after school, morning and afternoon, the process should be repeated for a longer time, and just before school, also, if the room can be warmed again quickly enough.* No fixed transom lights or immovable arched heads should be permitted to exist over the windows. . . . . [See paragraph number 94, (3) page 51].

"2. The sashes common in the more pretentious buildings should be rehung with rawhide cord or copper chain if necessary, and pulleys with friction rollers balanced so as to move with a touch, while in new buildings the size and weight of the sashes should be carefully kept down, no sash being over 3 feet wide or 1½ inches thick. Eyes must be fixed to the upper sashes and a pole and hook furnished to handle them with, or, still better, cords fastened to each sash hanging within easy reach and pulleys to raise or lower them at will, and the window frames must be perfectly made, with cherry beads, and looked after from time to time to see that all is in working order.

"3. Besides the general airings, in which all the windows are thrown wide open, it is possible and very desirable during three-fourths of the year to keep some of them partly open. If they extend to the ceiling, the upper part at least of the south windows, in rooms properly supplied with other fresh air inlets, may be pretty widely opened in the coldest weather without causing a noticeable draught. Such openings, if on the leeward side, often interfere with the action of extraction shafts by drawing to themselves the current of escaping air; but this, with care, might be minimized.+

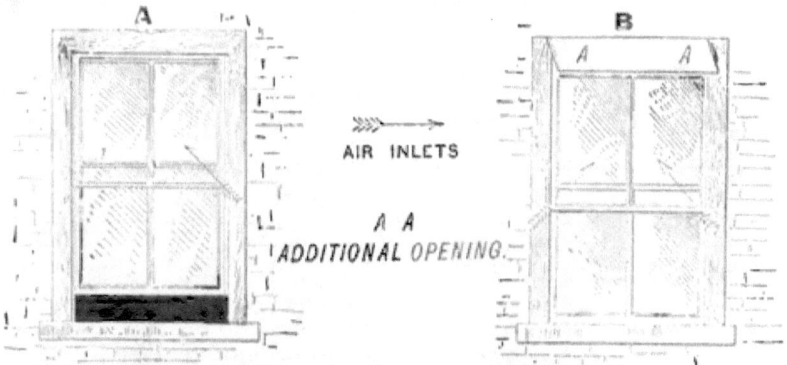

FIGS. 34 AND 35.— DOUBLE WINDOWS, WITH OPENING AT TOP OF ONE AND BOTTOM OF THE OTHER.

* For remarks on the construction of windows for ventilation, and "atmospheric washing" by those means, see paragraphs number 99 (h), page 56, and paragraph number 141. In regard to the hygienic value of the "school recess" see paragraph number 131.

+ Mr. J. Dearness, in his paper published in the Provincial Board of Health Report, also makes a suggestion on the subject. He says:—

"Windows should always be opened on the leeward side of the house, unless they are provided with appliances that will give the draught sharp upward deflection. The latter object is accomplished by placing a strip the length of the window frame, the width of the opening, and the thickness of the frame under the lower sash (see Fig. 34). The raising of the under sash accomplished in this way makes an entrance for the air between the sashes. It is less trouble to fix a strip of board under the top of the frame at a sharp angle with the top bar of the upper sash

"4. There are times, however, when the windows cannot be opened with safety. But means must be taken for ensuring the withdrawal of the respired air from the room in some other way.

108. Dr. D. F. Lincoln, in his report to the New York State Board of Health (1882) on School Hygiene, speaking of window "air inlets," says of them :—

"1. No apparatus that can be named will do so much good, at a very small cost, as the window-board—[that is] a plain piece of board, as long as the window is wide, and from four to eight inches in width. The lower sash is raised, the wood is inserted and the sash is shut down upon it. The air enters [as shown in Fig. 36] in a thin stratum, passing upwards between the upper and lower sashes in a nearly perpendicular direction, without causing perceptible draught. Fig. 36 (to the right) represents a double window

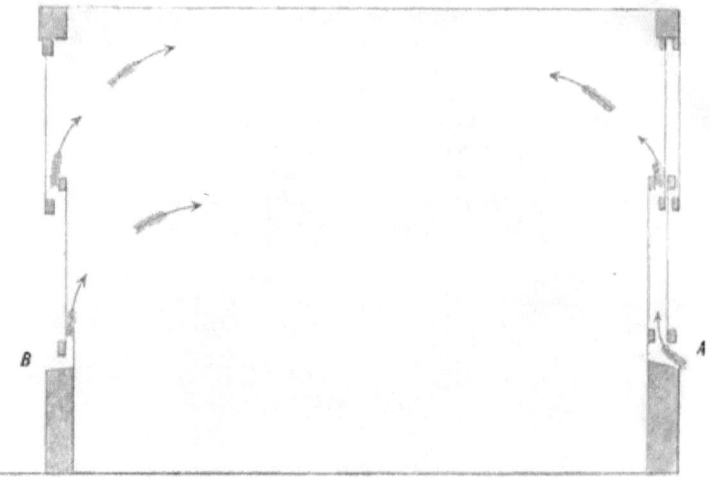

FIG. 36.—AIR-INLETS THROUGH WINDOW SASHES.

provided with a board, the air entering at A. This gives great protection from the cold, and also enables the air to enter the room slightly warmed by contact with the lower pane. All four sashes of double windows should be movable.

"2. At B [in the other window] there is a different arrangement for mild autumn or spring weather. The board is made wider, and is placed an inch or two from the sash, in such a way as to direct a current upwards. [The arrows indicate the direction of the currents entering the room through each kind of window when the boards are arranged as directed. See the Window illustrations in paragraphs numbers 99 (h) and 150.]

109. The writer then explains how often systems of ventilation fail, from want of judgment, or knowledge in the application of its principle which alone can make such systems successful, viz.: "The ascensive power of artificial heat." He says :—

(see 'AA' in Fig. 35), and then lower the sash. If the window is on the windward side the sash may safely be lowered an inch or two, or if on the leeward side pulled down to make an opening of eight or twelve inches."

Chap. XII.   School House Heating and Ventilation.

"1. Nothing is more common and more absurd than to see rough ventilation flues, 4 by 8 inches, built in walls without any provision for heating them, under the supposition that they will 'draw;' or to see tiny pipes, from the foulest places, introduced into chimneys which are cold half the time, in the expectation that the 'forced draught' which is imagined to exist there will suck up and carry off deleterious vapor as fast as a square yard of filth can generate it. All talk of 'forced ventilation' by means of a shaft without fans, [heat] or steam jets is misleading. The action of every such shaft or chimney, warmed or not, is precisely analogous to the movement of two boys balanced on a see-saw. If their weight is equal, neither moves; if one is slightly heavier, he descends and the other ascends, but his motion would not be fairly described by saying that he was 'forced into the air.' So with ventilating shafts; the column of air in them is balanced against a column of the same size and height outside of them. If the outer air is cold and that in the shaft warm, either from artificial heat or by communicating with a warm room, the latter column will be slightly lighter, because, being expanded, a given volume contains less weight. This difference of weight, if there is not too much friction in the chimney or elsewhere to be overcome, will incline the balance, and the air in the chimney will rise, cold air descending to take its place. The actual difference of weight between the column of air in a chimney 12 inches square and 30 feet high at a temperature of 100° Fahr. and an equivalent volume at 32° Fahr. would be 5 ounces; and this, deducting the friction of both the ascending and descending currents, will be the measure of the ascensive force of the air in the shaft."

"2. Without artificial heat the ascensive power is much less—infinitesimal often; and in summer the current in a chimney is at least half the time reversed, the evaporation of the hygrometric dampness of the masonry cooling the air within it below the temperature of the surrounding atmosphere.

"3. This force, feeble though it be, is all we have to depend upon, and it need hardly be said that all obstructions to its action must be avoided. The common cause of defective action is insufficient fresh air supply. . . .

* Dr. D. F. Lincoln, in his report on *School Hygiene*, published in the Report of the New York State Board of Health for 1882, says on this subject:—

"1. Few people are aware how small a quantity of air is actually drawn out of apartments by ordinary flues for ventilation. By 'ordinary,' I mean [an opening of the size of one or two bricks] (4x8 inches). . . . With a close grating . . . or register to obstruct a current at the bottom, or sharp angle at the foot, the inside roughened by protruding mortar and with only a [remote chance] of getting warmed with a smoke stack. . . Probably, in such a case, the rate at which the current moves, is something like a foot per second. The flue is drawing out a quarter or a half of a cubic foot of air per second—enough, perhaps, for *one person's* requirements. A large school room may often be seen provided with half a dozen or more of just such [sized] ventilating flues—enough for six or eight children. . . .

"2. School authorities should ascertain the real working capacity of the flues in their school houses, for the degree of deficiency can never be known in any other way. The anemometer will give a pretty faithful statement of the current actually passing through the flues. Analysis for carbonic acid in the air of the school room will give an excellent test. . . .

"3. A ventilating flue must draw, or it is worthless. This quality, which forms its sole merit, is aided by several other points, viz.:—

"(*a*) It should be as straight as possible from beginning to end. Curves and angles are very great obstructions.

"(*b*) It should not, as a rule, be horizontal, or descending in any part. . . .

"(*c*) It should be continuous from the beginning to where it discharges out of doors. . . ."

"4. In order, then, that there may be a flow of air through the room, not only must the withdrawing shaft be large, straight and smooth, that the inevitable friction of the air upon its walls may not materially obstruct the outward flow, but the inlet openings must be also ample and unobstructed, any hindrance to the inward flow being equally a check to the outward current. To use a homely illustration, the room to be ventilated may be imagined to be traversed by the lower end of a huge atmospheric roller towel. It makes no difference whether we pull one side down or the other side up to secure a movement; but if the towel is obstructed in any part of its course the whole is brought to a stand still. Recollecting also that to pull down a common roller towel actually takes more power than the whole force ordinarily available for moving the entire atmosphere of a large room, the total ascensive power of the usual ventilating shaft seldom exceeding one or two ounces, the imperative necessity for avoiding friction will be evident."

110. By way of practical application of the foregoing, the writer points out a remedy, which will be considered under the next heading.

NUMBER OF CUBIC FEET OF AIR PER CHILD.*

11. "In each room the area should be at least twelve square feet on the floor, and there should be at least two hundred and fifty cubic feet of air space for each pupil.— Regulations, 1885."

111. The application, in a practical shape, of the foregoing statements and illustration necessitates the consideration of the number of cubic feet of air which must be allowed per child in each school room. This involves the sizes of school rooms and the number of children which can be rightly accommodated in each of these rooms. This question also involves the height and floor area of the school room. While the area remains the same, cubic feet available may be increased by adding to the height of the room.

112. In order to minimize as much as possible the cost of school house construction, the Minister of Education has reduced the number of cubic feet of air for each child to the lowest point consistent with safety to the health of pupils in the school. (See Regulation No. 11 above.)

113. On this important question I give an extract from the report of a Committee on School Hygiene, published by the Provincial Board of Health in their report for 1883, as follows:—

"1. We are, no doubt, safe in affirming that in order to maintain the air of our school rooms at a proper standard of purity and render it fit for respiration, 1000 cubic feet of air space should be allowed to each pupil. This estimate is based on the following data:—

"(a) Air contains ·4 (CO) carbonic acid per 1000 volumes.

---

* See special reference to this matter in paragraphs, numbers, 10, 93, 114, 115 and 116.

CHAP. XII.   NUMBER OF CUBIC FEET OF AIR PER CHILD.   65

"(b) And if we adopt $\frac{3}{1000}$ cubic feet as our air space, then each individual exhales ·6 carbonic acid every hour per 100 volumes of air.

"(c) When three renewals of fresh air are effected every hour, each individual will, by respiration, add ($\frac{1}{3}$ of ·6) or ·2 of carbonic acid to the ·4 commonly contained in the air.

"(d) Consequently, the ratio of impurity will be represented by ·6 carbonic acid to 1000 volumes of air with three renewals each hour, and there will be no perceptible draught.

"2. But two questions here present themselves:—

"(a) What amount of carbonic acid shall be accepted as the standard of permissible impurity?

"(b) How many renewals of fresh air can be effected each hour without injurious draughts?

"(c) With regard to the first question, Dr. George Wilson records the result of numerous experiments which he had a share in conducting, and states the following general conclusions, which corroborate the experience of Parkes:—

"(d) That when the carbonic acid does not exceed ·8 in 1000 volumes of air, no tangible injurious effects upon the health can be detected, but when it reaches 1 in 1000 volumes of air the cumulative effects of breathing impure air manifest themselves."

"(e) Admitting this principle, the air space allotted to each individual pupil might be reduced to 500 cubic feet, with an efficient system of ventilation. The reason for this is clear. Because, if with three renewals of fresh air every hour ·2 carbonic acid is added as the respired impurity for one individual in 1000 cubic feet of air space, then ·4 of carbonic acid per 1000 will be added for the same individual in 500 cubic feet of air space under the same conditions.

"(f) With regard to the second question, if six renewals of fresh air can be effected each hour without injurious draughts, 500 cubic feet of air space may be sufficient for each pupil, since this will keep the standard at ·6 per 1000 volumes.

"(g) This can be accomplished by having inlets and outlets favorably placed, and judiciously managed, in a properly constructed room, according to some authorities. But skilful management in ventilating and warming is necessary in order to avoid injurious results.

"(h) Consequently, there is a possibility of confining pupils in an air space of 500 cubic feet, under certain conditions, without serious injury resulting from breathing impure air.

"3. Let us further ask ourselves, May we adopt a lower standard than 500 cubic feet of air space for each pupil?

4. In connection with this question, the system pursued in some schools in the United States of frequently opening doors and windows during school hours, in order to admit a free supply of outside air, is worth considering.*

---

* See extract in regard to this matter in paragraph number 107.

"5. The school authorities direct that a brief intermission shall be given to the pupils at the end of each hour. During this intermission, marching, gymnastics and other suitable exercises are practised by the scholars under the superintendence of the teachers. This plan has many advantages to recommend it. The physical exercises tend to promote the health of the pupils, and also greatly conduce to their comfort.

"6. The frequent exercises in pure air, with open windows, assist the pupils in throwing off the injurious effects of imperfect ventilation and confinement in seats.*

"7. Under such a system as this, energetically carried out, may it not be claimed that the perfect health of pupils can be maintained with a less air space than 500 cubic feet?"

114. The United States Book on School Architecture gives a practical application to its remarks on this subject, as follows:—

"The amount of fresh air which is allowed to hospital patients is about 2,500 cubic feet each per hour. Criminals in French prisons have to content themselves with 1,500 cubic feet per hour. Assuming that we care two-thirds as much for the health of our children as we do for that of our thieves and murderers, we will make them an allowance of 1,000 cubic feet each per hour. Forty-eight children will then need an hourly supply of 48,000 cubic feet. Definite provision must therefore be made for withdrawing this quantity of foul air. No matter how many inlets there may be, the fresh air will only enter as fast as the foul escapes, and this can only escape through ducts intended for that purpose, porous walls and crevices serving in cool weather only for inward flow. What, then, must be the size of the shaft to exhaust 48,000 cubic feet per hour? In shafts two feet or more in diameter, the velocity of the current varies with the height and with the difference in temperature between the atmosphere inside and that outside. In one 20 feet high, vertical and smooth inside, with a difference in temperature of 20 degrees, the velocity will be about 2½ feet per second, or 9,000 feet per hour; that is, it will carry off 9,000 cubic feet of air per hour for every square foot of its sectional area. To convey 48,000 cubic feet, it must have a sectional area of 5½ square feet."

115. Speaking on this subject, Hon. John D. Philbrick, LL.D. (referred to in note on page 51), in a letter to Hon. Henry Barnard, LL.D., of Hartford, Conn., a veteran educationist, and the first United States Commissioner of Education, says:—

"The highest pedagogical authority has decided that a school room should not exceed 27 feet in length or 20 in width—the story being 14 feet in the clear—this is for 49 pupils of the highest class.† The King William's Gymnasium in Berlin—one of the grandest school buildings in the world—in the building of which the highest authorities in architecture and pedagogy co-operated, provides for pupils of the highest class (18 to 20 years of age) 10·6 square feet of floor per pupil. The rooms in our [Public Latin and English High School, Boston], furnish 20·6 square feet to a pupil, very nearly double that of the Prussian edifice."‡

---

* In regard to this question of the "recess" and the advantages of it, see paragraphs, numbers 131 to 140, inclusive.

† See also paragraph number 94 (2), page 51.

‡ Dr. Philbrick when he refers to the Gymnasium in Berlin as "one of the grandest school buildings in the world," speaks with authority, as his Report on the school architectural display at the Vienna Exposition of 1873 will testify. It must be all that he has described it to be, as the

CHAP. XII.   SYSTEMS OF HEATING AND VENTILATION.   67

116. The Committee, which has recently awarded prizes for the best plans for a public school house in New York City, has given its opinion that "in each class room not less than fifteen square feet of floor area should be allotted to each pupil."*

SYSTEMS OF HEATING AND VENTILATING SCHOOL HOUSES.

"15. Care should be taken to arrange for such ventilation as will secure a complete change of atmosphere three times every hour."—*Regulations, 1885.*

117. The ordinary system of heating rural schools is by means of a stove. In most cases this system is unaccompanied by any plan of systematic ventilation, or of securing pure air from outside of the building. The door and windows (the latter often tightly shut) are often depended upon for such fresh air as they may casually admit to the school room. Efforts have been made by our Public School Inspectors to remedy this great evil, and to introduce a system of heating by hot air, a system the very principle of which is to displace the vitiated air already in the room. An example of an Inspector's success in this direction is furnished by Mr. David Fotheringham, Inspector of North York, in the shape of a plan of heating by hot air, which has been recently adopted, on his recommendation, by the trustees of a public school near Newmarket. Mr. Fotheringham has furnished a copy of this plan, which is inserted herewith (Fig. 34). He says :

---

very building in Boston, about which his letter was written, is "the grandest school building" in America. Its cost was upwards of three-quarters of a million of dollars, viz., $750,800. Dr. Philbrick, in his report to the United States Bureau on "City Schools in the United States," published this year (1885), refers to the City of London School" as a masterpiece of English school architecture." It is a classical school for 680 boys between the ages of 7 and 19, erected by the London City Corporation since the completion of the Boston edifice. The cost of the building, together with site, amounted to a million of dollars. No pains were spared to make this a model school house in all respects. Its magnificent site fronts the Victoria Embankment. The interesting details of this building are given in Dr. Philbrick's report (Circular of Information, No. 10, 1885), pages 168-171. Dr. Philbrick explains the reason of the superiority of the Gymnasium. He says :—"The highest authorities in architecture and pedagogy co-operated" in its construction That this co-operation was not an isolated case is evident from the following extract of his report on the school architectural display at Vienna in 1873: "Vienna knows how to build, and has built school edifices which are more durable, more safe, more convenient, more costly, and more beautiful than any Boston has yet built or is likely to build in the near future. The reason of this is, that in Vienna, when a school house is planned, it is done by the combined science and wisdom of the most accomplished architects and the most accomplished pedagogists. No mere whim of a school-master, and no mere whim of an inexperienced and uneducated architect, is allowed to control the design." Speaking also of the "Akademisches Gymnasium," in Vienna, Dr. Philbrick says :—" It was built by the Government . . . the design being the product of the best architectural . . . and pedagogical talent, working together . . . The lighting is perfect."

* Mr. W. R. Briggs, Architect to the Bridgeport High School, Connecticut, in describing that building, says : " In the corner rooms of Bridgeport School house, allowing 50 pupils per room, each pupil will have 20.50 square feet of floor space, and 266 cubic feet of air. In the middle rooms each pupil will have 21 square feet of floor space and 273 cubic feet of air. In the High School [large room, seldom used], allowing 200 pupils, each pupil will have 17 square feet of space and [being lofty] 447 cubic feet of air" per pupil.

"From the accompanying diagram (Fig. 37) you will understand my plan for ventilation. While I should avail myself of the ordinary means, through raising and lowering windows, and by ventilators in the ceiling and gable ends, I should have a shaft in connection with the chimney, composed either of a section of the chimney divided off by sheet iron (which would heat the air in the shaft), or by a pipe inside the chimney, either for the smoke or for ventilation.

"You will notice that I suggest cold air escapes at the floor into the basement, or into tubes opening outside the building ; higher up I suggest large ventilating registers to be under control of teacher."

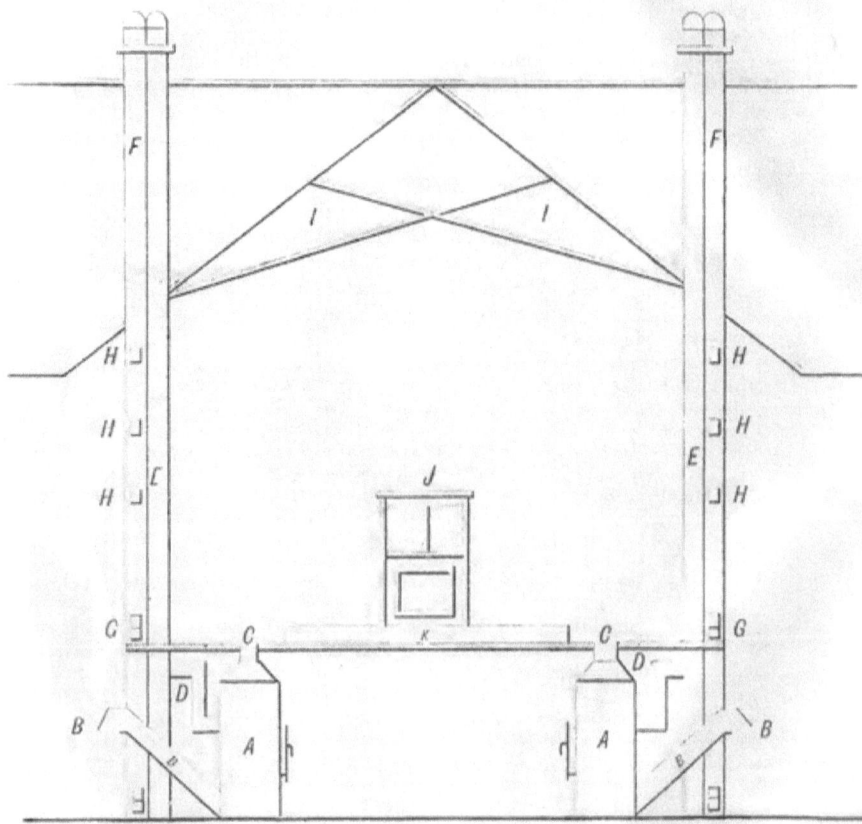

FIG. 37.—SECTION OF SCHOOL ROOM, SHEWING HEATING AND VENTILATING APPARATUS.

A.A.—Hot Air Furnaces.
C.C.—Hot Air Registers.
E.E.—Chimnies.
G.G.—Cold Air Escapes.
I.I.—Principal rafters— giving air space of 16 feet at sides, and 20 feet in the centre of the room.
J.—Glass door.

B.B.—Cold Air Duct.
D.D.—Smoke Pipes.
F.F.—Ventilation Shafts.
H.H.—Ventilation Registers.

K.—Teacher's Platform

CHAP. XII.   SYSTEMS OF HEATING AND VENTILATION.   69

118. Several of the other Public School Inspectors of Ontario have given their views on the subject of the heating and ventilation of schools, which are embodied in a report by a committee of themselves, of which Mr. John Dearness, of East Middlesex, was chairman. I insert the following :—

(1) Mr. F. Burrows, of Lennox and Addington, says :

"In ordinary country schools a good sized pipe with openings, enclosing the stove pipe and passing into the chimney will be found efficient for ridding the room of noxious air. The stove should be enclosed in a sheet-iron jacket, the chamber formed having communication with the pure air outside."

(2) Mr. E. B. Harrison, of East Kent, says :

"For the escape of foul air, ventilate into a flue built in the chimney as an air duct : also see Hodgins' "School Architecture," page 45, etc. For the supply of fresh air, air ducts and registers in the walls. The air to be obtained from as high a point as possible."

(3) Mr. Summerby, of Prescott and Russell, says :

"Fresh air admitted (from outside, not from cellar) through floor and heated as it passes the stove. Flue for exit of foul and cold air at end of room remote from stove."

(4) Mr. C. Donovan, Inspector of R. C. Separate Schools, suggests a :—

"**Ventilating** flue, side by side with draught flue of chimney, connecting by tube under floor with an opening, or register, at opposite end of the room ; fresh air admitted from outside by tube under floor. Operation : fire burning draws cold air from outside ; same in draught flue heats air in adjoining ventilation flue, causing it to rise and draw air from further part of room by tube under floor (first mentioned), thus creating a circulation."

(5) Mr. J. Dearness, of East Middlesex, in an elaborate paper on the "Sanitary Condition of Rural Schools," published in the Report for 1883 of the Provincial Board of Health, says :—

"Ventilation, by heating air drawn by flues from the outside in a chamber constructed round the stove, is an excellent method, but the chamber should be fitted to the stove in such a way as to expose part of the metal so that wet or cold feet can be dried or warmed at it. A register may be placed in the floor under where the stove will stand. The register draft may be fed by two zinc or galvanized iron pipes leading air from the outside, or by a matched covering of the joists between which the register is placed. In either case the flues, whether zinc or wooden, should be so close as not to allow the air 'from the cellar' to be drawn into the house.* Such a chamber as this needs a strong current of fresh warm air all the time that there is a fire in the stove.

"Speaking of ventilating flues, it may be safe to state as a rule, they are practically useless in rural schools unless they are warmed by the smoke flues passing through

---

* See remarks on air from the cellar in the extract quoted in paragraph 121, page 71.

them, or are heated in some other way. It is really surprising to find how many people think cold air and pure air are identical. I have several times, on complaining of the ventilation of the room, heard the command given to a pupil to 'close the damper.'

"One seldom sees an evaporating pan on the stove, or any other means adopted to maintain the proper hygrometric condition of the air in the school room. It is not generally known that external air at freezing point brought into a room heated to 65° or 70° requires at least four times as much moisture as it contained outside."

119. Dr. P. H. Bryce, Secretary to the Provincial Board of Health, has, at my request, sent to me the following suggestions as to the mode of determining the impurities in the air of a school room. He says:

(1) "The test of Dr. A. Smith is the ordinary one of measuring impurities by the milkiness caused in lime water through having the air of a room drawn into it, when carbonate of lime is formed by the *carbonic acid*, the air uniting with the lime. $(Ca O + Co_2 = CaCo_3)$.

(2) "This is done by having air drawn through the lime water by means of an asperator. The amount of Ca O (lime) in grains must be known, and the volume of air drawn through also calculated.

(3) "A rough way, but a very practical one, is to have a rubber ball containing a given number of cubic feet of air (calculated by the amount of water the ball will hold) compressed so as to drive the air through the lime water. This may be repeated any number of times. Turbidity of the lime water after a certain amount of air is driven through it will indicate contamination. The amount of lime-water and air necessary is readily calculated. This method may be practised by any school teacher. Supposing pure air produced no turbidity, the degree of contamination would be experimentally proved by the number of times the air of the ball is driven through the water. This can be easily determined by comparison with Angus Smith's tables found in 'Fox's Examination of Air and Water.'"

(4) "Professor Leeds . . . says . . . 'The air in winter is very dry, the moisture is squeezed out as the water is squeezed out of a sponge. But as you heat it you enlarge its volume again, and it sucks up the moisture just as this sponge does, and if you do not supply this moisture in other ways it will suck the natural moisture from your skin and from your lungs, creating that dry, parched, feverish condition, so noticeable in our furnace and other stove-heated rooms. Few persons realize the amount of water necessary to be evaporated to produce the natural condition of moisture, corresponding with the increased temperature given the air in many of our rooms in winter. Air taken in at ten degrees and heated up to seventy, the ordinary temperature of our rooms, requires about nine times the moisture contained in the original external atmosphere, and if heated to a hundred degrees, as most of our hot air furnaces heat the air, it would require about twenty-three times the amount in the external atmosphere.'"

120. Dr. Oldright, in a paper on School Hygiene in the Report of the Provincial Board of Health for 1883, discusses the question of "inlets" and "outlets" for air in school rooms. He says:—

1. "*Size of Inlets and Outlets.*—. . . There are 3,600 seconds in an hour, and we want 3,000 feet of air in that time, *i. e.*, five-sixths of a foot per second for each indi-

vidual; this, with a current of five feet per second, will require our 'hole,' or inlet, to be one-sixth of a square foot, or twenty-four square inches per individual; and the same to let the air out. If heated it will have to flow more rapidly, and it may more safely be allowed to do so.

2. "*The relative position of the Inlets and Outlets.*—Their relative positions will vary much, according to varying circumstances; among which may be mentioned the shape and size of the room, the season of the year, the mode of heating. . . . There are certain general principles, which, if strictly remembered and carried out, will help us much in the consideration of details in each special case. There are four of these general principles that must never be lost sight of:

(*a*) " The air brought in must be distributed throughout the whole of the breathing space.

(*b*) " It must be of a suitable temperature, when it comes in contact with the inmates, and of a suitable degree of humidity.

(*c*) " It must be pure.

(*d*) " Hot air is lighter than cold.

3. " It is of great importance to bear in mind these four principles; it will be found that every defect in ventilation is due to a violation of some one of them."

121. In a note to paragraph 124, I have pointed out the necessity for bringing in fresh air from outside at points three or four feet above the ground level. (See Fig. 38.) In no case should the air for a heating furnace, or for a stove jacket, be taken from the cellar. The "reason why," is thus graphically given by Dr. Lincoln. He says:—

"It cannot be too often repeated that the purity of cellar air lies at the foundation of the purity of house air. The danger of severe and sudden illness lurks in cellars, as often as in sewers. The common practice in regard to cellars is to bury the drain under its floor, . . . in short, there are few uses of a menial sort to which it is not put. The cellar is often without a proper floor, often is very dark and close for want of windows. . . . To these sources of pollution (for darkness is one source) add the fact that in cold weather a powerful outside pressure exists, forcing air into the cellar and thence into the upper parts of the house."

HEATING AIR FROM OUTSIDE BY A STOVE IN THE SCHOOL ROOM.

122. Although a furnace, or heater, in the basement (as illustrated by Mr. Fotheringham, Fig 37 on page 68) is considered the best means of heating school rooms, yet the plan mentioned (on page 72) by other inspectors of heating them by stoves in the school room, is the most common plan. Without certain arrangements and precautions, this is a very faulty and unhealthy system. As a general rule, no provision is made for ventilation by the constant production of warmed air and the exit of vitiated air. The stove is often placed at one end of the room, and the pipe is carried over the heads of pupils—to their serious detriment. The only

way to obviate these defects (if a stove must be used) is to place it near the north-east angle of the school room, and bring fresh cold air in from the north side of the school house, in the manner illustrated in the accompanying simple diagram (Fig 38) which (with new features added) has been adapted by me from one in an American school report :—

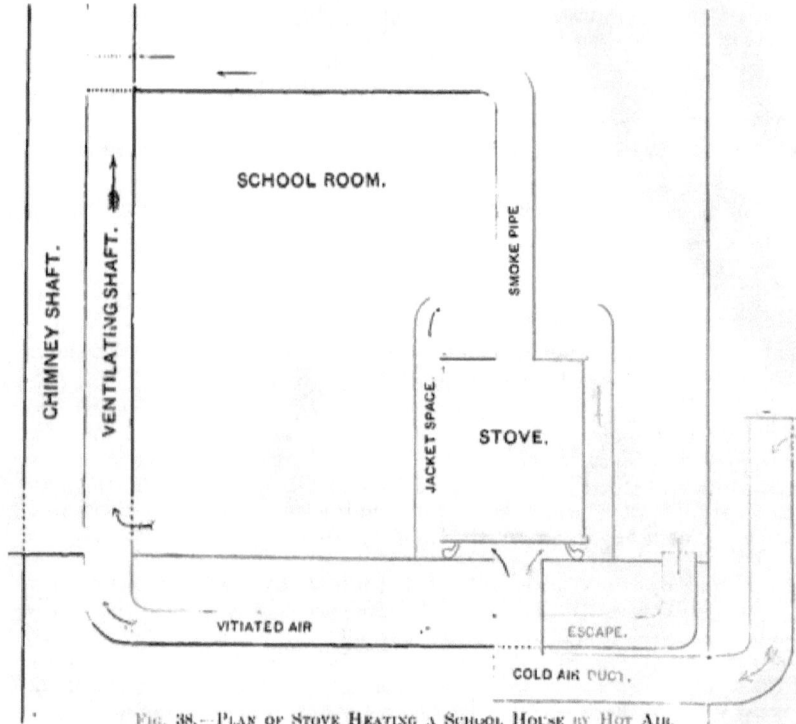

FIG. 38.—PLAN OF STOVE HEATING A SCHOOL HOUSE BY HOT AIR.

123. It will be noticed, that in Fig. 39 (next page) one of the escapes for vitiated air is under the teacher's platform ; others are under the desks, etc. In no case should the fresh air be admitted from the ground level outside; but it should be invariably taken from about three or four feet above the level, through an air duct, as shown in the diagram above (Fig. 38), with wire gauze covering or a register.*

124. The following illustration shows what would be the practical working of such a system in the school room :

---

* In a report on school hygiene by Dr. D. F. Lincoln, approved by the N. Y. State Board of Health, he says :—"There is much carelessness about the source of air which is drawn [from outside, and sent into the school room. The ground may, it is true, be a pure and unoffensive bit of turf, but that is an unusual condition of the school yard. Bad air, malarial air, is known to settle upon the ground in many cases. . . . Sundry unpleasant elements in the surroundings of school houses are at the ground level. As a rule, openings for drawing the outer air into the house had better be at points above the children's heads, and covered with wire netting."

CHAP. XII. AIR CURRENTS IN HEATING AND VENTILATION. 73

FIG. 39.—SECTION OF SCHOOL HOUSE, SHOWING AIR CURRENTS AND VENTILATION.

125. The Cottier system of ventilation, recently adopted in the school houses of Portland, Oregon, has worked well. It is based upon the use of the attic as a warm air, or expansion chamber, out of which there is an ejector through the roof into the open air. From a detailed account, furnished to me by Mr. T. H. Crawford, City Superintendent of the Portland City Schools, I have condensed the following summary on the subject :—

The tin flues for vitiated air used (four in each room) are ten inches by four in size. They reach from the rooms to the attic, and extend a few feet above the attic floor. To ensure a strong draft, hot-water coils (or hot air through flues will answer), are placed in the attic, some feet above the floor. To enforce a more rapid ventilation, a gas burner is placed in each tin vitiated air flue, five feet from the floor, with a glass door opposite to it in the flue. The attic, or expansion chamber, is made airtight, and all doors leading to it closed. Hot air pipes are placed under the windows, etc., on two sides, or on one side and end, of the room. The warm air rises and receives the cold air from one-inch openings at the top of the windows and by transoms over doors. These openings are so small and numerous that no sensible draught can occur.

126. A Medical Commission was appointed in Germany not very long since, to report on certain questions relating to school house construction. In the report which the Commission prepared, it was laid down that 2,120 cubic feet per hour for each pupil was the minimum quantity of fresh air which should be supplied to each pupil. The Commission stated that—

(1) "In the best arranged ventilating shafts, of metal, fitted with gas-flames, stoves, or other artificial means for promoting the draught, the upward current of vitiated air will occasionally reach a velocity of a thousand feet per minute, in cold weather, although the average, in ordinary cases, is rarely more than five hundred feet and generally much less; so that to ventilate a room containing sixty pupils thoroughly, it should have an outlet shaft of four square feet or more, in sectional area, to be even capable of such ventilation as is essential.

(2) In regard to lighting, the Commission rejected the theory of unilateral illumination,—following in this respect the French authorities. In the language of the report, "it is practically impossible, even with lofty and narrow rooms, to obtain sufficient light by this method. In cases where openings can only be made in one wall, the report requires that the width between the windows shall not exceed three-fourths of that of the windows themselves, and that the width of the room shall not be more than five feet greater than the height of the windows, which would restrict it in such cases to about eighteen feet as a maximum. Light from the rear is admissible, but is not recommended, and windows facing the pupils are prohibited. Walls of neighboring buildings painted white and reflecting the sunshine into the school room are very injurious, and the owners should be persuaded or obliged to paint them of a dark color. The inside face of the walls of the school room itself is to be painted blue or bluish white, and the ceiling pure white. Artificial light should be used without hesitation on dark or short days. It is more dangerous to work by insufficient daylight than by gaslight."

127. In concluding this important portion of the subject, it may be well to emphasize the statement in the recent report (for 1885) of the Board of Public Instruction for the City of Albany, N.Y., that :—

"No system of ventilation is automatic. And unless teachers will themselves attend to the regulation of the temperature of their rooms, and act upon the directions ordinarily given, not even the most perfect system of heating and ventilation will keep the room free from foul air, and the inmates from discomfort."

FIRE-ESCAPE DRILL AND READY EXIT

303. "In every school-house consisting of more than one story, the pupils should be regularly trained in the fire drill, in order to prevent accidents from the alarm of fire."
—*Regulations, 1885.*

128. Dr. John D. Philbrick, in his recent report, says truly :—

1. "The disasters which have been caused by fire panics in large schools have suggested. . . (1) Fire proof furnace and boiler rooms ; (2) fire escapes ; (3) safe

CHAP. XII.   FIRE-ESCAPE DRILL AND READY EXIT.   75

staircases ; (4) and the outward opening [as is the law in Canada] of the main doors of entrance. . . . The fire drill . . . is not only an effective safeguard against the danger of panics, but also a good gymnastic exercise. He quotes the report on the subject, made on the Rochester (N. Y.) schools, by the Springfield (Massachusetts) School Superintendent, as follows :—' At a given signal (which is heard throughout the building) the pupils in every school room rise instantly to their feet, form in line, as they have been previously instructed, . . . and pass rapidly, in double lines, down the stairways and out into the yard,—those on the first floor going out first, and those on the second and third following in order. Upon reaching the yard they form into line again, facing the building, ready for orders. . . . This exercise . . . is now used in many places as a pleasant and safe kind of recreation.' . . .

2. "In the schools of Vienna . . . this manœuvre . . . is executed in three different ways. . . . In case of a fire in the neighbourhood (signal No. 1) the pupils place their books in their satchels, put on their outer garments, and leave the class room in groups of four. If the danger is imminent (signal No. 2) the books are left, the outer garments rapidly put on, and the class room is left as before. . . . In case of extreme peril (signal No. 3) the books and clothing are left, and the exit is made immediately in groups."

129. Mr. A. Scott Cruikshank, Head Master of the Hess School, Hamilton, thus describes the system of fire drill adopted in that school:—

"The alarm is either the continuous ringing of a bell, or the natural cry of 'Fire! Fire!!' Immediately boys are detailed to open doors and take their several stations. At the same time teachers are ordering the prompt dismissal of their classes. On the word, 'One,' all stand ; 'Two,' they form in line, two deep ; 'Three,' they move out with the teacher, girls first, as the boys generally close up better in the rear. Instructions are given to pupils that they are in no case to pass the teacher, whose brisk walking keeps the smaller pupils running as fast as is consistent with safety. Arrangements are also made for each class to keep its own side of the stairway, and move on independently of other classes preceding or following. This prevents danger of crossing each other's course, or otherwise interfering in the general haste to reach the door. Our three stories—600 pupils—have been cleared in less than two minutes."

130. In the note to paragraph 85 I have pointed out the necessity for constructing doors and other entrances to open outwards, as required by law, and to make them, and the stairs and passages as wide as possible. The pupils should also be drilled to make rapid exit from the school house, so as to prevent a panic in case of fire, etc. Dr. Oldright, in the report for 1883 of the Provincial Board of Health, says :—

"Good broad stairs, doors opening widely outwards, and efficient fire escapes, are some of the requirements needed. In this connection, I would desire to allude in terms of commendation to the action of some of our school authorities in exercising the pupils in fire drill, and would express the hope that this action may become more general, as also the systematic sanitary inspection of schools, etc."

CHAPTER XIII.

HYGIENIC VALUE OF THE SCHOOL RECESS.

§. "There shall be a recess of not less than ten minutes each forenoon and afternoon, and at least one hour shall be allowed for recreation during the middle of the school day—Regulations, 1885."

131. The great object aimed at, or rather the two-fold object aimed at in prescribing the usual "school recess," is (1) to afford the pupils a few moments of relaxation from the studies of the school room for "atmospheric washing," and (2) to give the teacher an opportunity to open windows and doors, and thus secure to the school room a free ventilation and pure air.

132. It is not necessary to discuss here the importance and necessity for a recess for these purposes. They are self-evident. It is desirable, however, to ascertain the best method of dealing with the question of the "general" or "open" recess, so far, at least, as it relates to the well-being of the pupils. The other object of the recess, (*i.e.*, ventilation of the school room), is easily effected as soon as the pupils leave the school room.

133. Unless there is some covered shed or large spare room to which pupils can go, it is a question, whether it is wise to allow the boys and girls to rush from the warm school room into the open air, especially on a wet, cold, or snowy day. On this point, the Superintendent of the Albany schools, in his report for 1884, makes the following remarks. He says:

"You all know how often pupils . . . rush into the school-yard at recess time, bareheaded and ill-clad, in defiance of the mandate of teachers, and expose themselves to rain, sleet or snow, or to the extremes of cold and heat, and return to the school-room chilled through, or with clothing saturated with moisture, and thus incur the risk of contracting severe, and perhaps fatal, illness. It will not do to say that teachers should take precautions against these dangers. The time-table calls for a "recess," the pupils are eager to play, the teachers are glad to be free, and the weather will not be scanned very closely—it is hard to draw the line—errors of judgment are frequent, and the exposure follows."

134. The Superintendent then goes on to point out other drawbacks to the "open" recess system. One is "the danger arising from the sudden return of children, glowing with exercise, to a school room whose temperature has been purposely reduced for sanitary reasons." Another is the injury often arising to the younger children from the rough play of vigorous boys and girls. A third is the opportunities which the open recess affords for the exercise of petty tyranny "so dear to too many boys and girls."

CHAP. XIII.   HYGIENIC VALUE OF THE SCHOOL RECESS.   77

135. It may be said that these latter evils may be controlled, if not prevented, by the presence of a teacher. True, but unfortunately the pupils are, in too many cases, left to take care of themselves. Dr. D. F. Lincoln, in the report of the New York State Board of Health, speaking on this point, says :—

" Some teacher has to watch the pupils while in the school yard ; and this must be, especially for ladies, one of the most difficult and distasteful parts of the teacher's duty." The Superintendent of Albany, says :—" To add this task to the complete and varied duties entailed by courses of study and school regulations, would be to sacrifice valuable time now devoted to more important interests."

136. In many American cities and towns a new system, in place of recess, has been adopted—that is, of allowing short intervals for mental rest—* of having calisthenic, or like exercises, in a large spare room, or in the shed or yard, while the rooms are being ventilated ; and lastly, by giving two full hours at the noon intermission.† Amongst the reasons urged for this change, are the following, by Dr. D. F. Lincoln, of the New York State Board of Health. He says :—

" Troops on the march are accustomed to halt at the end of each hour. A school should also have its halting times (and once an hour is not too often), when the air may be renewed by a quick and brief opening of the windows, while the pupils go through some light gymnastics."

137. Dr. Yeomans, in a paper on school hygiene, in the report for 1883 of the Provincial Board of Health, speaking of the school recess, virtually endorses the principle of the new American system in the extract quoted from his paper in paragraph number 140.‡

138. The School Superintendent of Albany thus sums up an elaborate argument in favor of the new system of school recess. By it, he says—

" Valuable working time is gained ; discipline is eased ; petty tyranny [in the play yard] is abolished ; sweeter voices and pleasanter manners result ; the moral influences of the abode are bettered, or rather the opportunities for evil influences are largely reduced ; family convenience is better served ; habits of study are strengthened ; desirable pupils attracted ; the per cent. of attendance raised ; and, as a consequence of all these results, children are made wiser, happier and better."

* Speaking of such an interval of "mental rest," Mr. T. H. Crawford, Superintendent of the Portland Schools, Oregon, says :—" Any skilful teacher can have a five minute social in the school-room, during which the fullest freedom can be permitted to the pupils. It is the weak teacher who dares not relax the iron rule of 'attention, eyes front !'"

† Mr. Crawford, Superintendent of the Portland Schools, Oregon, in referring to the satisfactory working of the new system, says—speaking of the lengthened noon intermission—"The time gained in the morning by the present plan, added to the noon intermission, enables most of the pupils to reach home more easily, eat their dinners quietly, and return to school without racing ; teachers have also an opportunity for some relaxation at noon," instead of being "compelled to remain in the buildings to supervise the pupils," etc.

‡ The arguments advanced in favor of this new system are answered by Drs. Philbrick, Harris and Hancock, in paragraph number 140, and page 78.

139. In the report of the Committee of the American Council of Education, on "Hygiene in education," laid before the Council in 1884, the question of school " recess, or no recess " is discussed. The medical testimony adduced is, in a sanitary point of view, in favor of the ordinary school recess every hour, " until," as one of them adds, " our school buildings are perfect in the matter of providing pure air." The opinion of the committee is mainly in favor of the old system. They say :—

1. "Occasional exposure to inclement weather is far less to be dreaded in the pure air, than is the constant exposure in poorly ventilated school rooms.

2. " If doors and windows be thrown open during in-door exercises, exposure is greater than when children go out of doors properly protected by their wrappings, which they do not think of putting on in doors. . . . In addition, they lose the vivifying effect of abundant sunlight and pure air. Even with doors and windows open, the air of the school room is not changed while the [pupils'] little laboratories of carbonic acid remain in quickened activity within the room."

140. Dr. John D. Philbrick, in his report published in 1884, lays down the following rules for " School recess."

1. " In infant schools, recess is necessary after the lapse of one hour, and a change of position and physical exercise should be allowed as often as once in thirty minutes. For pupils twelve years of age and upwards, there may be allowed a session of two hours without recess, but such a session should be broken in the middle by some physical movement or rest.

2. " The regulations of the City of Cincinnati respecting school hours and recesses, is perhaps as judicious as can be devised for the same latitude, and it has borne the test of [ten years'] experience.*

3. " In some [schools] the teachers are forbidden to deprive children of recess as a punishment, and it would be well if this rule were universal. . . .

4. "The universal conviction of the utility and necessity of recess has prompted school authorities to provide as large lots as possible on which to erect school houses. Immense sacrifices have been made for this object in all the more advanced educating countries. The extent and character of the play ground have, in fact, come to be a tolerably reliable indication of the liberality of a community in respect to its schools.

5. "The recess question has been set in its true light by Dr. William T. Harris, in an able and sound piece of pedagogy, written in 1884—the substance of which is summarized as follows :—(1) 'The recess has been established by the practical wisdom of the past school management, and it seems to meet certain physiological requirements

---

* The regulation made November, 1874, directs (1) that "the hours of tuition and study shall be as follows: From September 1 to July 1, 9 a.m. to 12 m., and from 1.30 to 4 p.m., with fifteen minutes' recess each morning and afternoon. [The younger classes], grades E and F shall be dismissed each afternoon at 3 p.m. (2) For the better guarding of the health of the pupils of grades D, E and F, (lowest primary grades) . . . there shall be allowed to the pupils of these grades, at the close of each recitation, the space of five minutes for calisthenic exercises in the room during which time the room shall be ventilated. . . . Passed in November, 1853."

of the young and growing individuals for whom it is appointed, in a better manner than any other device yet proposed can do. (2) The moral argument used against recess applies against association in coming to school and in returning from it, as well as remaining at the noon intermission. . . . Recess is the only interval when the pupil is out of school, and yet completely under the control of the teacher. The teacher has no other opportunity so good as the recess wherein to teach the pupils to treat one another politely, by repressing the rudeness, personal violence, profanity and [other evils] that will break out, and must be eradicated. . . .

6. "The reactionary movement against recess is probably owing, in the main, to the . . . substitution of women for men as teachers and principals, even of large mixed schools. . . The [necessary] oversight . . . of school boys at recess, is a duty . . . which women . . . usually perform with reluctance. . . . The true remedy, . . is the employment of a sufficient number of judicious male teachers to manage the recess of boys in a proper manner.

7. "Dr. Hancock, School Superintendent of Dayton, Ohio, in speaking of this subject in his report, remarked as follows:—'The best ventilated school building ever constructed is not so well provided with pure air as all out doors; and no throwing up of windows, no free gymnastics in doors, can compensate for spontaneous and exhilarating exercises in the unrestricted atmosphere of the play ground.'

8. "In the latest report (1883) of Mr. George Howland, School Superintendent of Chicago, an experiment in the mode of conducting recess is mentioned, as follows:— 'In many of the schools a change has been made with excellent results; the pupils of the first floor [or division, etc.] passing out and returning to their places, and then those of the second and third in succession. By this method time is saved to the individual classes, the smaller children are less liable to be injured by the larger ones, the school play ground is much less crowded, and both teacher and pupil relieved from much annoyance.'"

CHAPTER XIV.

WINDOWS AND LIGHTING.*

14. "*The windows (both sashes) should be adjusted by weights and pulleys and provided with blinds.—Regulations, 1885.*"

141. The question of the admission of light to a school room is an important one, and should be carefully considered in the planning of a school house. The consensus of opinion of experienced physicians and

---

* The opinions, on this subject, of the Brussels Congress of Education in 1880, of the United States Commission at Washington in 1882, and of Dr. J. D. Philbrick in his official report on City Schools to the United States Bureau of Education in 1885, are exceedingly valuable and important. See paragraphs numbers 93, 94 and 146.

competent observers is that light should be admitted so as to fall on the left hand side of pupils; that it should be admitted from **one side of the room only**—and that the south side. These rules cannot always be followed, so that other suggestions have to be made. They are to the effect that if light is admitted from both sides of a school, these sides should *not* be the **east** and west, but the **north** and south. The reasons will be found in the following extracts. Mr. J. Dearness, in his paper published in the Report for 1883 of the Ontario Board of Health, quoting authorities on this subject, says:—

"A few years ago it was not uncommon to place windows at the end of the room in front of the children. But the increase of hygienic knowledge . . . has almost removed this evil. In Germany, by law, light must be admitted either from the ceiling or from one side only, and the seats and desks must be placed so that when the pupils are reading or writing the light will be supplied from their left. The height of the window-sills from the floor should always be as great as possible. The nearer the approach to lighting from the roof the better. Robson, the best English authority on the subject, says the sills should never be less than five feet from the floor, and may be even more, with advantage both for lighting and ventilation. Dr. Linell, of Norwich, Conn., who has studied the subject very carefully, says that windows should always be on the *side* of the room, and there should be thirty square inches of window space to every square foot of floor space. He has recently examined the eyes of 700 school children varying from seven to eighteen years, and found that only 61 per cent. of them had normal vision. In that number there were 87 cases of myopia [short sightedness]; the ratio of myopia increasing with the ages of the scholars. Much responsibility rests on the teacher in this matter. Diseases of vision from causes peculiar to the school room most frequently arise from improper postures of the body, and wrong habits of holding the book. The teacher must be blamed if the children, during the writing exercises, crouch over the desk until their noses are within two or three inches of the slate or paper."

142. Hon. A. J. Rickoff, late Superintendent of Schools in Cleveland, Ohio, in a paper on "A plan for a School House," said:—

"It will be seen that the principal and, generally, all the light necessary for each school room is admitted on the side of the room which is to the left of the pupils. . . . This is looked upon as the special advantage of the plan."

143. Mr. W. R. Briggs, School Architect in Connecticut, in a paper published in the report for 1882, of the State Board of Education, says:—

"All eminent writers on School Hygiene have called attention and dwelt with much stress upon the importance of abundant light being properly distributed in our school rooms. That the light should come from the left side and be introduced at nearly right angles to the floor line is an established rule among those versed in school matters. In the Bridgeport School House the window-stools have all been kept 4' 0" from the floor, and the window openings are carried up to within one foot of the ceilings. The size of the windows, taken collectively, equals, in the corner rooms, one-sixth of the floor space, allowing 50 pupils per room, and provides 434 square inches of glass per pupil." (See paragraph, number 94 (3), page 51.)

144. In a paper on "Country School Houses," by Mr. J. Hess, published in the report for 1882, of the **State School Superintendent of Michigan**, he says:—

1. "In Dr. Buk's Treatise on Hygiene, we are assured that short-sightedness, dimness and darkness of sight are increasing generally in Germany, Russia, America and England [among children attending school] and we are assured at the same time that the defective eyesight is much greater where school rooms are poorly planned regarding their window arrangements.

2. "Too much (or not enough) light, cross lights, or light falling at a low angle [i. e., afternoon western light] into the school room, . . . are all injurious to the scholars and teachers, and should, therefore, in planning a school house be properly considered. . . A few simple rules may be taken as a guide, and in case of too much light, it must be toned down by the use of blinds, shutters, or window shades."

145. I have condensed and simplified these rules, as follows:—

1. Light from above a person's eyes is the most natural, and accepted by all as the best; the most unnatural light is from below.

2. For writing, drawing, or working, light from the left hand side is almost indispensable, while light from the right hand side is not desirable except for reading or oral exercises.

3. I add here a caution suggested by Dr. John D. Philbrick, in his recent report on Schools in the Cities of the United States. He says:

"When the unilateral principle [of lighting] was first applied in Boston, some twelve years ago, . . . the fatal error occurred . . . of making the rooms too wide (i.e., 36 feet), whereas the width should not have exceeded 25 or 26 feet."

4. Light from the back and left hand together is not injurious, but at times the pupil's back light, which the teacher faces, may be inconvenient to him. From the back and right hand side together, and from the front, light should never be tolerated in a school room.

5. The size of windows collectively should measure not less than one-sixth of the floor surface of a school room.

6. Reflected light from above should be promoted by making a clear, white ceiling. Reflection from the walls in front and at the right hand side should be avoided, by giving the walls a neutral tint.

7. Blackboards should never be placed between the windows as they

would receive a very unfavourable light and would strain the eyes of the pupils too much.

146. The writer of the United States book on School Architecture says :—

1. "It is agreed by all authorities that the most comfortable and wholesome light for the eyes is that coming from one side of the room, without interfering crosslights from windows in the opposite side or from front or rear, and it is furthermore desirable that the light should come from a group of windows, or a single one, rather than from a succession of them separated by wide piers, which cast annoying shadows."

2. "For writing or drawing the light should come from the left, not exactly at the side, but a little in front; then neither the head, the right hand, nor the pen will cast a shadow on the paper. For reading, the light may come from either side, indifferently, but should be a little back. In arranging schools containing four or more class rooms on a floor, only two modes of lighting are practicable : one, by windows in two adjacent sides ; the other, by windows in one side only.

3. "Of these two alternatives, the latter should always be chosen. The confusion of crosslights at right angles to each other and the shadow of the head thrown forward are injurious to the eyes. . . . The openings in the one illuminated side should be numerous and large, or the more distant portions of the room will be too dark, and the seats should be so arranged that the light in each room will fall upon the left side of the pupils.

4. "Under this arrangement, with lofty rooms and large openings, the comfort of the eyes is at its highest point, and it is therefore compulsory in all German schools of every grade."

147. In applying these principles of window construction to rural school houses of the ordinary kind, difficulty might be experienced, especially as it is so desirable to obtain a free circulation of air in the school room during recess. The writer just quoted makes the following suggestions to meet the difficulty :—

1. "Next to the north aspect, the steadiest light, as well as the greatest amount of sunshine, is derived from one due south, and while a south window receives the sun nearly all day the year round, the angle at which it enters is so great that the annoyance from it in hot weather is infinitely less than from the horizontal rays which stream through an east or west window [the latter at a low angle]. For this reason, a south exposure is both cooler in summer and warmer in winter than an eastern or western one, and while it secures the largest possible aggregate of sunshine, a south window needs less shading with blinds or curtains than any other, except one facing north.

2. "On the whole, therefore, although some authorities hold a different opinion, the writer believes that the main room or rooms in small school buildings will be best placed with the longer axis directed due east and west, and lighted by windows in the north and south sides only."

CHAP. XIV.   THE SHAPE AND SIZE OF THE WINDOW SASH.   83

148. After further pointing out the objections to light in a school room from the east, and particularly from the west, the writer sums up thus :—

1. "With north and south lighting, all these difficulties vanish. The condition of the room in relation to the furnaces will in winter be always the same, the north side being constantly cold and the south side warm, so that a single stove or furnace placed near the north wall will at all times diffuse its heat uniformly through the room. In summer the north windows will never need shading and those on the south only to a small extent. In winter the range would be much greater, though the annoyance would be at that season be far less. In any case, the shading of a small fraction of the window surface will cut off all the rays which can possibly strike upon any desk, while a west window can be effectually shaded only by closing every crevice through which a horizontal beam can pierce. . . .

2. "Nor is the sunning of the room by south windows less effectual, but more so, than by east and west. The most obvious influence of sunshine upon the atmosphere of a room is to set it in motion.

3. "Both chemical and mechanical effects are produced with greater energy by the noonday beams than by the heating, though lifeless, rays of a horizontal sun, and the circulation between the north and south sides of a room lighted from both quarters is the more active and constant by reason of the great dissimilarity in their condition, one being always shaded and cold and the other always warm."

THE SHAPE AND SIZE OF THE WINDOW SASH.*

149. The following suggestions in regard to the window sash by this writer are valuable. He says :—

1. "The height of the room will be generally about 12 feet, and if the windows are carried to within 6 inches of the ceiling the total height of the frame will be $7\frac{1}{2}$ to $8\frac{1}{2}$ feet. So high a sash ought not to be over 3 feet wide, and both parts should be well counterbalanced, by weight, so as to encourage their frequent opening. A heavy or badly hung sash will rarely be opened, from the simple physical inability of teacher and children to manage it. A ring should be screwed into the top of the upper sash, and a pole and hook provided to operate it. The glass should be in rather small lights [8x10] for cheapness of repairs and English 'double thick' on all exposed sides. . . .

2. "The cheapest device of all for blinds is the ordinary shade, which should be made of stout holland, never of paper or painted cotton, and strongly and accurately hung. This has the objection of shutting out air in summer as well as sun, and a modification may be used, consisting in a short [movable] curtain, only half the height of the window and moving up and down by means of the ordinary brass pulleys and endless cords, to which it is secured along the edges by rings and hooks.

3. "It is important that the sills of the windows should be as much as four feet above the floor. If less than this, they cause a glare in the eyes of the pupils sitting near them. . .

---

* See the Window illustrations on pages 56, 57, 61 and 62.

4. "To compensate for the height of the sills above the floor, the window heads should be carried as close to the ceiling as the construction will admit [as shown in Fig. 40.]*

FIG. 40.—WINDOW OPENING, SHOWING OUTSIDE CORNICE.

Four inches is all the distance which need generally be given in frame structures, and even in brick buildings the sash can be carried nearly as high, as will be seen further on. The illumination of the ceiling so obtained is of the greatest value, the light reflected from it being peculiarly soft and grateful to the eyes, while the proper ventilation of the room is greatly assisted by making the windows as high as possible."

HOW TO DEAL WITH WINDOWS WITHOUT PULLEYS.†

150. Dr. Oldright, in his paper on "*Healthy Homes*," published in the report for 1883 of the Provincial Board of Health, makes the following suggestions for dealing with windows without pulleys, by—

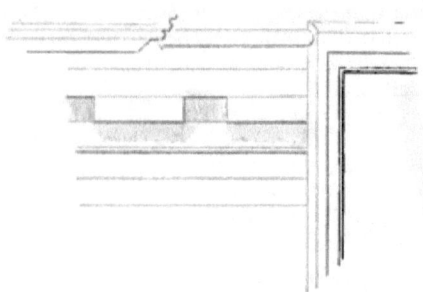

1. "Having a piece of board nailed on to the top sash of the window, slanting upwards, to direct the current in that direction.

2. "Raising the lower sash and filling in the space left under it by a piece of board, as shown in the accompanying diagram. The air gets in through the space left between the lower part of the upper sash, and the upper part of the lower one.

3. "A board placed just inside the lower window frame will act in the same way when the latter is slightly raised.

4. "Placing wire screens in spaces of entrance of air. Sometimes they are tacked to the window frames and folded up when the windows are closed.

5. "By louvred openings.

6. "By double panes, with an open slit at the bottom of the outside one and at the top of the inside one, thus giving an upward current."

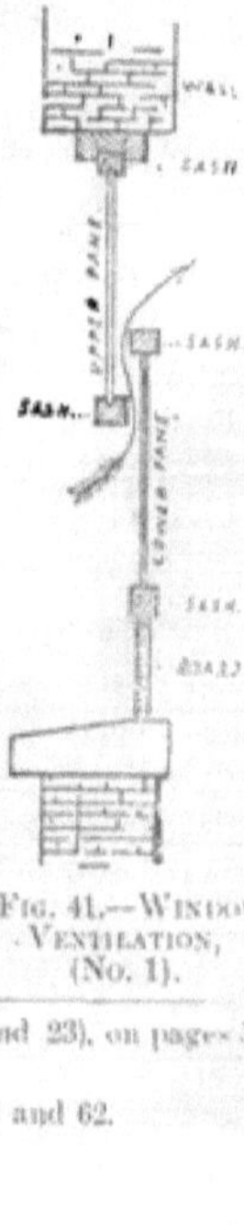

FIG. 41.—WINDOW VENTILATION, (NO. 1).

---

* See also the practical illustrations on this subject (Figs. 20, 21, 22 and 23), on pages 56 and 57.

† Illustrations of how to deal with such windows will be found on pages 61 and 62.

151. Dr. Oldright **also** suggests **the** following means **of** "inviting, directing,** breaking **up and** distributing currents of air entering **a** room."

7. **"By** various **perforated and louvred bricks, such** as the Sheringham **valve, and** Jenning's air brick.

8. **"By** a box **running from** side to side **across the ceiling of the** room, and **perforated** with numerous small openings. Sometimes a **diaphragm is** placed to divide it midway, thus making both **inlet and** outlet.

9. "By perforated cornices **running around the room**."

10. **"By** Tobin's tubes**, which are flues,** bringing fresh air **from out doors and rising** up from **the floor**, discharging **it upwards** at a slight distance **overhead."**

CHAPTER XV.

SCHOOL SEATS AND DESKS.

152. The Departmental Regulations **on the subject of** seating **the pupils are** specific. I give them here **entire, as follows :—**

(a) **The seats and desks should be** so arranged **that the pupils may** sit facing the teacher. Not **more than two pupils should be allowed to sit at** one desk, but single-seated desks are **preferred.**

(b) The height **of the seats should be** so graduated **that pupils of different sizes may** be seated with their **feet resting firmly upon the floor. The backs should slope backwards** two or three **inches from the perpendicular.**

(c) The seats and **desks should be** fastened **to the floor in rows, with aisles of suitable width** between **the rows ;** passages, at **least three feet wide, should be left between the** outside **rows and the side and the rear walls of the room, and a space from three to five** feet wide, **between the teacher's platform and the front desks.**

(d) **Each desk** should be so placed that **its front edge may project** slightly over the **edge of the seat** behind it. The desk should **be provided with a shelf** for pupil's books, **and the seat should slope** a little towards **the back.**

(e) **A sufficient number of** seats and desks should be provided **for** the accommodation of all the pupils ordinarily in attendance at the school. There should be at least two ordinary chairs in addition to the **teacher's chair.**

(f) The desks should be of three different sizes. The following dimensions are recommended.

AGE OF PUPILS.	Chairs or Seats.			Desks.			
	Height.		Slope of Back.	Length.		Width.	Height next Pupil.
	Front.	Rear.		Double.	Single.		
Five to Eight years	12 in.	11½ in.	2 in.	36 in.	18 in.	12 in.	22 in.
Eight to Ten years	13 "	12½ "	2 "	36 "	18 "	12 "	23 "
Ten to Thirteen years	14 "	13½ "	2½ "	36 "	20 "	13 "	24 "
Thirteen to Sixteen years	16 "	15½ "	3 "	40 "	22 "	13 "	26 "

PRACTICAL SUGGESTIONS IN CARRYING OUT THE REGULATIONS.

153. These regulations are so full and explicit that little is needed but to add to their force and value by quoting the opinions of experienced educators and other competent authority on the subject.

154. The writer of the United States work on School Architecture, already quoted, says:—

1. "The proper way to plan a school building is to determine the number and size of desks and the width of aisles and platform first of all, then to construct the walls to inclose just the space desired and no more; not, as sometimes occurs, to fix upon some haphazard dimensions for the room, and when it is ready cram the desks in somehow, the result being that the room presents in one place large useless spaces and in another aisles so narrow that the children can only squeeze through them sideways.

2. "Taking things as they are, not as they perhaps ought to be, the majority of ungraded schools are likely to use double desks, and the plan will be first laid out for such, leaving till later the arrangement to suit the single desk seating.

3. "The dimensions of double desks vary according to the maker, and the utmost economy of floor space will be secured by determining upon the kind to be used before commencing the construction of the building.

4. "The folding seat desks, which are desirable, especially for young children (because they allow the pupils to stand upright in their places, turn the seats back, and in that position take part in various calisthenic or other exercises), occupy a little more room from front to rear than the old kind, but are made somewhat shorter, the average length being 40 inches for the double seat, and the floor space from back to back 30 inches.

5. "The aisles between the rows of double desks should be two feet wide.

6. "The teacher's platform, or a space for the desk if a platform is not used, will be five feet wide, and three feet, at least, must intervene between the front of the platform and the front row of desks.

7. "Three and a half, or, better, four feet, should be allowed between the rear seats and the wall, and aisles next the side walls are necessary, three and a half feet wide, if blackboards are to be placed there, or three feet wide if they are dispensed with.

8. "There should be not more than four rows of double desks. The advantage of shortening the school room by increasing the width, is more than counterbalanced by the annoyance to the teacher of constantly turning the head in trying to take in a wide angle of vision.

9. "Three rows of desks would give a room of better form still for seeing, hearing, and economical construction; but the width of such a room, amounting to 20 feet only inside the finished walls, would not be sufficient to allow the drawing out of large classes in front or rear of the desks. With four rows, therefore, as a standard, the desks, being 40 inches long, will require 13 feet four inches; three two-foot aisles between them will add six feet; and the two side aisles, each three and a half feet wide—seven more; making the total width of the room, inside the finished walls, 26 feet four inches.

10. "For the depth, the teacher's platform will take five feet; the front aisle, three more; eight desks, at two and a half feet each, will add 20 feet; and the rear aisle, which must be four feet if there is any possibility of adding recitation rooms on that end, brings the total to 32 feet and gives seating capacity for 64 pupils of all ages.

11. "If it is decided to use single desks, which are rapidly superseding double ones, in the more intelligent communities, the dimensions of the room will, with advantage and economy, be somewhat different.

12. "The usual width for aisles between single desks is 18 inches; six rows of desks, therefore, at two feet each, with five aisles, at one and a half feet, will take 19½ feet; two side aisles will, as before, add seven feet, making 26½ feet. To accommodate 60 pupils, there will be 10 desks in each row, at two and a half feet of floor space for each, which, with eight feet in front and four in rear, gives 37 feet for the depth of the room."

155. Dr. J. D. Philbrick, already quoted, lays down the following rules in regard to a proper system of School-Room seating. He says:—

"In a square room [and in other rooms in proportion] the best arrangement of the desks would be in the form of a parallelogram, the lowest side being parallel to the teacher's platform, 56 desks, a fair number for a primary school room, arranged in such a room in the best manner, the desks being one foot and a half in length, which is sufficient, the centre aisle being two feet wide, and the two aisles sixteen inches each, a width sufficient for all practical purposes, would occupy a floor space of 22x15 feet, or 330 square feet. A room 28 feet square and 13 feet high, with 784 feet of flooring, would be sufficient for the accommodation of the 56 primary pupils seated as above described, supposing the daily attendance to be 50, and allows a little over 200 cubic feet of space per pupil."

156. Dr. Oldright has sent to me a table of figures, showing the dimensions of seats and desks suitable for pupils of different heights. He states in the work on *School Hygiene*, that—

"The height of the pupil is measured every six months in France and some other European countries, and they are adjusted to their seats in a satisfactory position. Dr. Guillaume states that the seats at the Ecole Première were altered in this way, with excellent results. Rules have been laid down, giving measurements to guide teachers in regulating seats for children.

157. This information and that which precedes it (from United States sources) show the increased care which is being exercised by modern educationists in various countries, in the important matter of seating children at school. What a different state of things from the backless forms and rude benches of a few years ago! The table prepared by Dr. Oldright will be found in Chapter XX. of the Manual on *School Hygiene*.

CHAPTER XVI.

IMPORTANCE OF SCHOOL-ROOM DECORATION.

158. A book of this kind would scarcely be complete, did I fail to say a few words on a subject, the importance of which has of late years forced itself upon the attention of thoughtful educators and educationists alike. The lasting impression—pleasant or often the very reverse of pleasant—which the school house itself and its surroundings have made upon the minds of children, is well known. The fact that this is so is a matter of universal experience. That early impression has proved itself to be a potent factor, not only in colouring the imagination of the pupil in after life, but in vivifying the pleasant or unpleasant memories and associations, as the case may be, of early school days.

159. A wonderful change for the better has taken place in the character of the schools and in the *personnel* of the schoolmasters, since the time when the latter were so graphically and truthfully sketched by Goldsmith and Dickens. It is a matter of fact, however, that the traditions of the past still linger amongst school boys that school was not as desirable and attractive a place as it might and should have been.

160. Nevertheless, it is but just to the modern teacher to state that efforts are being made, and successfully made, to render the interior of the school attractive and pleasant, and to make the associations of school life itself pleasant. Arbor day, Author's day, noted Educators' day, etc., are designed to accomplish the latter, while as yet the effort to secure the former is confined almost exclusively to the teacher, and that by means of local school museums; or by pictures, flowers and ornaments in the school room.

CHAP. XVI.   SCHOOL ROOM DECORATION.   89

161. In his report on City Schools in the United States, Dr. J. D. Philbrick has devoted a chapter to this important subject. It is so full of information and suggestion that I give it entire as follows:—

1. "Closely allied in purpose and utility with the idea of the school museum is the idea of the decoration of the school room. This idea is rapidly becoming general. City school rooms totally destitute of objects intended for decoration are, perhaps, exceptional. We find almost everywhere that the most naked and unadorned have at least a plant in the window, a picture on the wall, or a decorative drawing on the black board. The profusion of plants in some primary school rooms gives them the air of a conservatory. In visiting the schools of Pittsburgh several years ago, I was greatly charmed with the taste everywhere displayed by the teachers in the decoration of their school rooms with plants and flowers.

2. "Nearly twenty years ago New York set an example in the decoration of school halls with numerous busts and engravings. Subsequently a committee was appointed by the educational department of the Social Science Association, to consider and report on the subject of the decoration of school rooms, with a view of introducing an æsthetic element into the educational system of the United States. The immediate result of this movement was the decoration of the hall of the girls' high school house in Boston, which was then building, with a selection of casts from antique sculpture and statuary. The expense of purchase, transportation, and placing of the casts was met by the subscriptions of a few members of the association, with the aid of some persons not members, on condition that the hall should be finished at the expense of the city, with special reference to the plan of decoration which had been decided upon. For a series of slabs from the frieze of the Parthenon an architrave was constructed resting on Doric pilasters. Between these pilasters the walls were painted of a color suitable as a background and brackets or pedestals of proper form were provided for the busts and statues. Casts, if selected to express the highest laws of form and the purest types of beauty, could hardly fail to produce a favorable effect upon the mental and moral training of the young, especially if associated with their studies; that is, their daily efforts to improve themselves. The collection was not made for a single school or for a single city, but for every school and every town or village where a similar attempt to extend the culture and beautify the environments of our educational system is possible. The theory of æsthetic culture in schools, upon which this plan of decoration was based, is essentially the same as that propounded and so ably advocated by M. Ravaisson, of France, under whose direction a series of magnificent phototypes of antique sculpture and statuary have been prepared for the decoration of schools.

3. "If the school room is adorned with works of art, the pupils' ideas are associated with things of beauty as well as utility. Ruskin, in speaking of the decoration of the school room with busts and paintings, says: 'How can we sufficiently estimate the effect on the noble mind of a youth, at the time when the world opens to him, of having faithful and touching representations put before him of the acts and presences of great men; how many resolutions which might alter and exalt the whole course of his after life, when in some dreamy twilight he met through his own tears the fixed eyes of those shadows of the great dead, unescapable and calm, piercing to his soul, or fancied that their lips moved in dread reproof or soundless exhortation.'

4. "Falling upon this fine passage of Ruskin, at once so poetic in conception and so sound in doctrine, I was naturally reminded of a striking example of the realization

of the idea it recommends—the most striking example, perhaps, which has come under my observation—namely, the decoration of a remarkable Jesuit school of the highest order which I visited some years ago in the city of Paris. Everywhere in this great establishment, which is shut in from the outside world by high walls even more effectually than Girard College, were decorative representations in sculpture, paintings, engravings, and sun pictures of men and deeds, calculated to inspire the pupils with the spirit of the institution and stimulate them to the utmost efforts for the attainment of the objects which it proposes. It is, perhaps, scarcely necessary to say that this example is rendered especially important by the fact of the well known success of the Jesuit schools in determining the character of their pupils.

5. "It is remarkable that in the country where such an example was found in a private establishment, and in a country so eminent for its cultivation of art in all its departments, almost nothing had then been done through the agency of the common schools to promote by the indirect means under consideration the moral and æsthetic culture of the masses of the people. Since that time, however, a very important movement has been made on this line of improvement. At the suggestion of M. Buisson, director of primary education, the Minster of Public Instruction appointed a Commission on the decoration of schools and art for schools,* consisting of thirty eminent men. This commission was charged, in general, with the duty of studying the means of introducing into the system of instruction in all its grades the æsthetic education of the eye. The results of the labors of the commission, which were extended over the period of a whole year, were summed up in a remarkable report to the Minister by Charles Bigot.†

6. "This report begins by presenting in a felicitous and forcible manner the argument in favor of combining in education the cultivation of the sentiment of the beautiful with the sentiment of the true and the sentiment of the good, maintaining that nothing great has been done on the earth except by the effect of one of these three sentiments, each having its apostles, its heroes, its martyrs. A grateful posterity places equally in its Pantheon, and honors with a pious worship, scholars, artists, saints, these glorious examples of humanity.

7. "The cultivation of the sentiment of the beautiful by means of poetry and poetic and artistic literature was never wanting in the schools of the higher grade. More recently provision had been made for extending culture in this direction by the general introduction of instruction in music and drawing. The especial task of this commission was to devise ways and means for improving, as far as practicable, æsthetic education through the eye, not by specific, direct instruction set forth in programmes, but by the operation of the environments of the school and the artistic character of its appliances. These environments and appliances were considered by the commission mainly under four heads: (1) The æsthetic character of the school building, including its artistic ornamentation, both exterior and interior; (2) the furnishing of objects of art for the observation and study of the pupils, such collection of objects belonging neither to the appliances nor to the architectural decoration, constituting the school museum of art; (3) the rewards of merit and prizes; (4) illustrative apparatus, and particularly the

---

* Commission de la décoration des écoles et de l'imagerie scolaire; appointed June, 1880.
† Presented April 11, 1881; printed in the Manuel Général de l'Instruction Primaire, July 23, 1881.

department of transparencies. Here it was deemed that scientific accuracy alone was not sufficient, but must be accompanied with elegance of form and harmony of colour, so far as the nature of the object would permit. This commission examined and reported upon the propositions and objects submitted by publishers and artists, comprised under the four categories above enumerated.

8. "The essential outcome of the labors of this large and very able commission, besides the valuable contribution to pedagogy comprised in the observations and discussions of their report, was the institution by the Minister of a permanent commission for the promotion and perfecting of this department of public instruction.

9. "This interesting movement of the educational administration of France has attracted the attention of educators on the other side of the Channel. Some time ago a committee was appointed in Manchester, England, ' to remedy the deficiency of English school arrangements in the means of awakening a sense of beauty and an interest in art.'

10. "The functions assigned to this committee, which are similar to those of the standing French commission, are as follows :

(1) "'To negotiate with art publishers for the purchase of prints, photographs, etchings, chromolithographs, etc., on advantageous terms, and to supply them at the lowest possible price to schools.

(2) "'To reproduce from time to time, by one or more of the processes familiar to engravers and printers, carefully selected examples likely to have a large circulation.

(3) "'To print a descriptive catalogue and price list of the examples which the committee are prepared to recommend to the notice of schools.

(4) "'To present to schools, in special cases and as the funds of the association shall allow, small collections and books explanatory of them.

(5) "'To arrange various loan collections, to be placed at the disposal of schools on such terms as may prove convenient.

(6) "'To bring together a number of examples to be exhibited in a suitable place as a tentative model of a standard collection, the collection to consist of (*a*) pictures of the simplest natural objects, birds and their nests and eggs, trees, wild flowers, and scenes of rural life, such as town children seldom see and country children often fail to enjoy consciously until their attention is specially called to them ; (*b*) pictures of animals in friendly relation with human beings, especially with children ; (*c*) pictures of the peasant and artisan life of our own and foreign countries, incidents of heroic adventure, etc. ; (*d*) pictures of architectural works of historic or artistic interest ; (*e*) landscape and sea pieces ; (*f*) historical portraits ; (*g*) scenes from history ; (*h*) and last, but by no means least, such reproductions as are available of suitable subjects among the numerous works of the Italian, Dutch, and modern schools.'

11. "More recently an association has been organized in London, with Ruskin as president, with a similar object in view, namely, ' to bring within the reach of boys and girls in our board and other schools such a measure of art culture as is compatible with their age and studies.

12. "The committee on drawing of the Boston School Board (Mr. C. C. Perkins, chairman), in their report for 1883, called attention to those movements in Manchester and London, and suggested the desirableness of organizing for the same purpose an ' art, for schools, association' in that community. In this connection the committee remark :

13. "'We hold with the English committee that 'a love for the beautiful is, perhaps, only second to religion as a protection against the grosser forms of self-indulgence, and that it can best be kindled at an age when the mind is especially susceptible to the influence of habitual surroundings;' and on these grounds we look for the sympathy, although we cannot ask the co-operation of the board in our proposed effort to found an art for schools association in Boston; and this, not only because the decoration of school-house walls with good prints and photographs will bring good influences to bear upon the pupils, but also because these will materially aid teachers of history, geography, and natural history as objects of reference. The decoration of the exhibition hall of the girls' high school with casts and the prints hung up in certain grammar and primary school class rooms shows that the masters and teachers are, in many cases, alive to the importance of the subject, and ready to aid in any well organized effort to promote its further development.'"

14. "The committee might have appropriately referred, in this connection, to more recent and not unimportant contributions of works of art to the schools under their charge, the most valuable of which decorate the main vestibules of the new school houses of the Latin and English high schools. In the latter a beautiful group in marble, the subject being, 'Flight from Pompeii,' has been placed by one of the earliest graduates of the schools (Mr. Henry P. Kidder). In the Latin school vestibule stands a fine marble statue by Mr. Richard S. Greenough, a Latin school boy, which was procured by the graduates of the school to honor those who had honored her, and especially to commemorate those who had fallen in defending their country. This statue represents the alma mater of the school resting on a shield which bears the names of the dead heroes, and extending a laurel crown to those who returned from the war."

162. The subject of school room decoration and the beautifying of school grounds has been extensively discussed in the educational journals, chiefly in the United States. The following from the *New England Journal of Education* puts the matter in a striking and practical light:

"This is a generation quick to interest the young through pictures. The brightest minds are busy with efforts to devise the most interesting pictures for the young. We carry the idea into our instructions. Object lessons are popular as June picnics. The lyceum has caught the fever. With the speaker comes the stereopticon. The lecture must be a picture gallery. Some are introducing the blackboard into the pulpit. The chalk competes with the pen. Ideas must be pictures, they tell us. Now look at that gaunt, bare, uninviting school house. What kind of a picture are we putting before the young? They will surely receive an impression of some kind, and of a lasting kind. Because the natures we are dealing with are so susceptible, and through life will go stamped with what we impress them, therefore we should have school houses and school furnishings as tasty and beautiful as possible. What about the neglected yard before that old education box? Plant a tree, or trees, there. Put vines at the base of the walls; and may no penny squeezing committee say the vines will rot the shingles when the roof is reached. Slate the roof, sir! What a pretty spot the school yard becomes! And as the scholars grow up to make homes for themselves, their trained interest in the picturesque will repeat itself in their tasty surroundings."

CHAPTER XVII.

PLANS FOR RURAL SCHOOL HOUSES.

163. The style of the exterior of a school house must necessarily be left to the choice of the school trustees. Its external appearance is always a matter of taste. Of course the exterior must in a large degree be made to harmonize with the requirements of the interior, and as to whether the building shall consist of one or two stories. All that is attempted in the following plans is to suggest variety, and to provide for a choice of some of the latest and best of the school houses which have

FIG. 42.—DESIGN FOR A RURAL, OR VILLAGE, SCHOOL HOUSE.

been erected in the United States, or are suggested. Some of these plans have been prepared for the Department; others are adapted by me from other sources and approved by the Minister of Education, so as to make them more suitable for adoption in Ontario.

164. Before consulting these plans, with the view to a choice, the trustees concerned would do well to refer to paragraphs numbers 93 and

94 (pages 50-52), in which the requisites of a good rural school house are pointed out by authorities of large experience.

165. The first design for a rural, or village, school house (Fig. 42) has been modified and adapted by me from an American source. It is of a modern style of school house, and can be built of wood or brick, or both combined. The design shows a neat finish of the upper part of the building in sheeting, with pointed ends. This sheeting should be tongued and

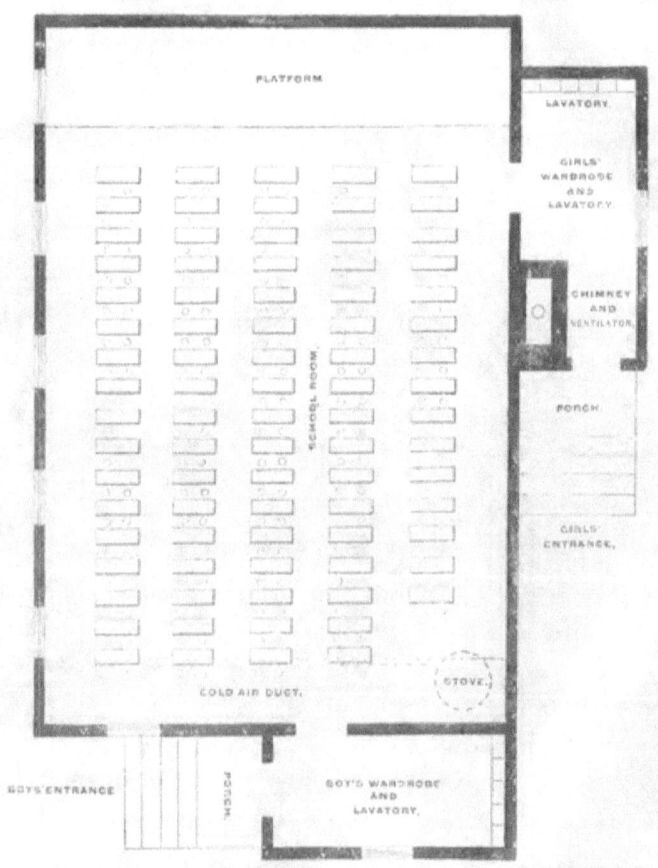

Fig. 43.—Ground Plan of Rural, or Village, School House.

grooved, and might be battoned, if desired, as shown in paragraph, No. 171, page 99. The building is well set back in the school grounds, and has a lawn in front and play grounds at the sides, as shown in block plan, Fig. 15, page 48. The entrance for girls is shown in this design—that for boys will be seen in the above ground plan, Fig. 43.

CHAP. XVII.   PLANS FOR RURAL SCHOOL HOUSES.   95

166. The ground plan, Fig. 43, is intended to be suggestive, and may be adopted, or not, at the pleasure of the Trustees. By placing the entrances for boys and girls at the side and the end of the building, the great desideratum can be secured of having the light coming in from only one side of the school house, and that the left hand side, as strongly recommended in Chapter XI, paragraph number 93 (pages 50 and 51). This plan has been modified and adapted from one suggested by Mr. Julius Hess, of Michigan. Lavatories for boys and girls have been added, and the seats have been differently arranged. A ventilator has been placed in the chimney, as will be seen in the plan, so as to ensure rapid ventila-

FIG. 44.—DESIGN FOR A RURAL, OR VILLAGE, PRIMARY SCHOOL HOUSE.

tion in the school room. The cold air duct from the outside to the stove (or furnace, as the case may be) is also shown in dotted lines.

167. Fig. 44 is also a neat design for a rural school house, or a village primary one. It was prepared by Messrs. Terrell and Morris, of Columbus, Ohio, and is kindly furnished by Hon. Le Roy Brown, the Ohio State School Superintendent. The architects say—"The school house when erected cost $2,000. It was built of brick and stone, with pressed brick arches, slate roof and slate blackboards. It is a one room building (as

shown in the vignette ground plan at the right hand upper corner of the design). The light comes in from the left and rear. It will seat fifty pupils. The flues are used for ventilating stoves by taking fresh air from the outside by a register in the floor directly under the stove. [See Figs. 38, 39 and 53]. There are two flues in the chimneys, one for smoke and the other for ventilation, with register at the floor line."

168. The general outline of this design can be adapted to ground plan, (Fig. 45), so as to construct a village school house with two rooms on the ground floor. This ground plan was also suggested by Mr. Hess, but has

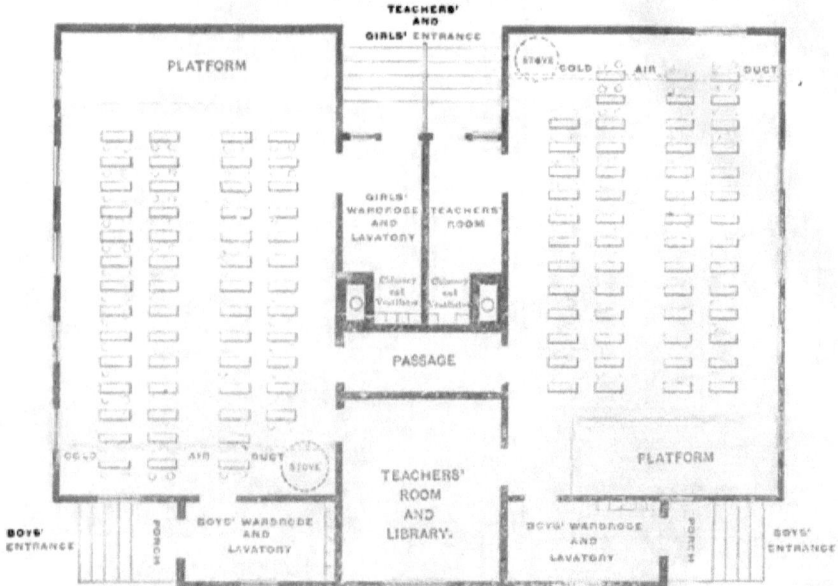

FIG. 45.—GROUND PLAN OF SCHOOL ROOMS FOR A VILLAGE GRADED SCHOOL.*

been modified by me in several important particulars, especially in the entrances, and in providing a teacher's room and library, also wardrobes and lavatories. The light also, as will be seen by the plan, comes only from the left hand side of the pupils, as has already been suggested. The passage from one room to the other is placed just outside of the teachers' room, as shown in the plan. The teachers' and girls' entrance is at one side of the plan, and those for the boys of each division at the opposite side. Each has separate wardrobes also.

169. Fig. 46 is a design which was prepared for the Department. It is intended to illustrate a style of exterior for a rural or village school house different from those previously given. It is intended to be a frame

---

* Dr. J. D. Philbrick, in his report on city schools, speaks favourably of this style of school room arrangement—that is, of having school rooms on each side of a central corridor. It combines many excellencies which cannot be introduced in the single school room plan.

CHAP. XVII.   PLANS FOR RURAL SCHOOL HOUSES.   97

building, but with ornamental bracings on the outside, so as to furnish some relief to the monotony of the ordinary "clapboarding" of a frame building. The ground plan adapted to this design is shown in Fig. 47.

FIG. 46.—DESIGN FOR A RURAL OR A VILLAGE SCHOOL HOUSE.

170. This ground plan explains itself, as its principal features are indicated on the plan itself. It is the ordinary adaptation, with a few improvements, of the "single room" system, which invariably provides for light coming from both sides of the school room. Separate entrances

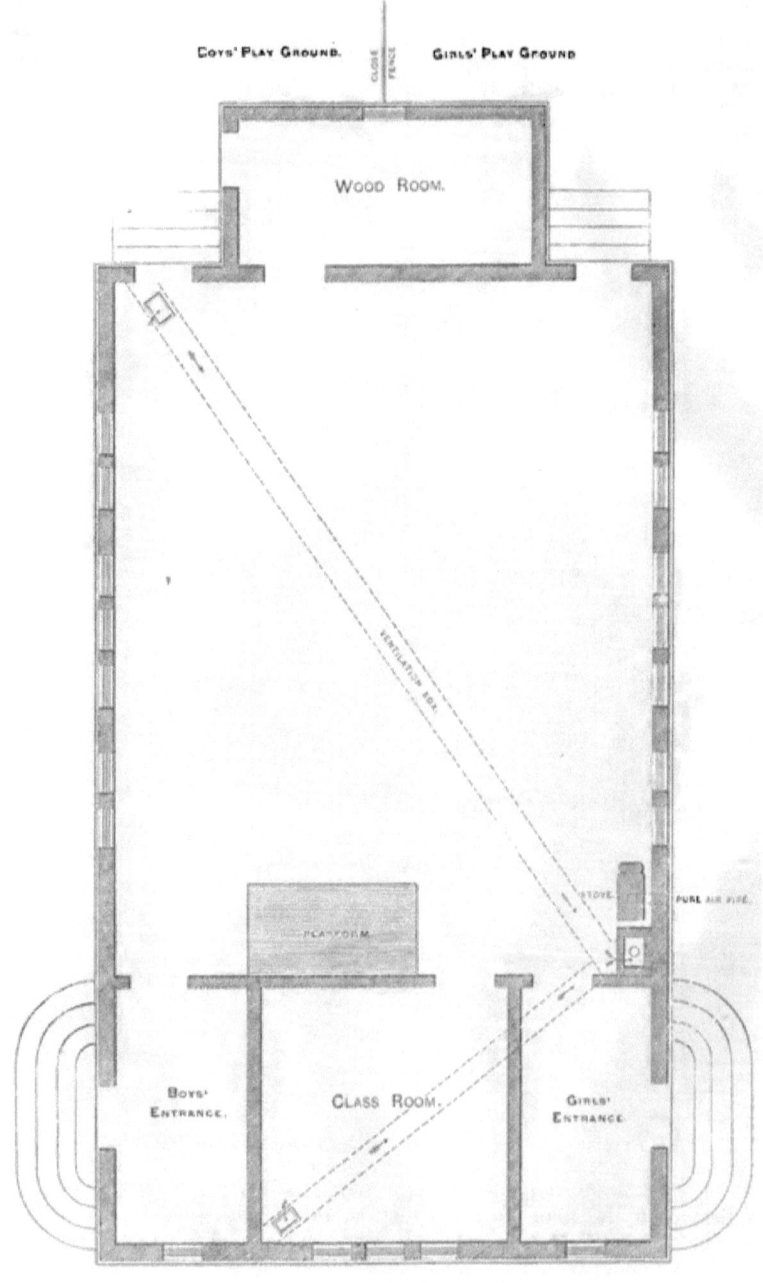

SCALE 4 FEET TO ONE INCH.   GROUND PLAN.
FIG. 47.—ADAPTED TO THE DESIGN SHOWN IN FIG. 46.

CHAP. XVII.   PLANS FOR RURAL SCHOOL HOUSES.   99

and exits for the pupils—boys and girls—are provided. In the modern school house these are considered indispensable, for reasons given in the appropriate chapter. The "entrances" can also be used as wardrobes, and the class room, for a teacher's room and library, if not otherwise required. The wood room is at the rear of the house, as are the doorways leading to the playgrounds.

171. The design which has been suggested for this style of school house is also suitable for a building enclosed with vertical matched boards, nailed to sill and plate, and to horizontal "inter-ties." In such a case, the

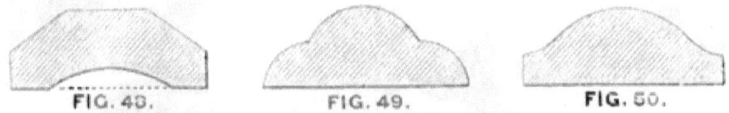
BATTENS FOR OUTSIDE VERTICAL MATCHED BOARDS.

joints would have to be covered with "battens," of any one of the patterns shown in Figs. 48, 49 and 50. These battens, (as suggested by Mr. T. M. Clark, the writer of the United States work on school architecture):—

"should have the tops bevelled or rounded, or they will curl up and admit water; and it is well also to hollow out the back with a plane to assist it in hugging close to the joint," as in fig. 48.

FIG. 51.—DESIGN FOR A RURAL OR VILLAGE SCHOOL HOUSE.

172. Fig. 51 is a design (prepared for the Department) of a frame house for a village graded school. It is simple in its construction, and, by way of relief to the plainness of the design, provides for an ornamental bracing on the exterior, as also shown in the design given in Fig. 46.

173. The **ground plan** for this **school** house design provides for **two school rooms of a graded** school, as **does the** ground plan (Fig. 45), but **in it the arrangement is quite** different. **Either** plan can be adapted to the **design** (Fig. 51). **In the** ground plan **(Fig.** 52), there are a boys' and a girls' **entry to each school** room. **It also shows** the points from which the air

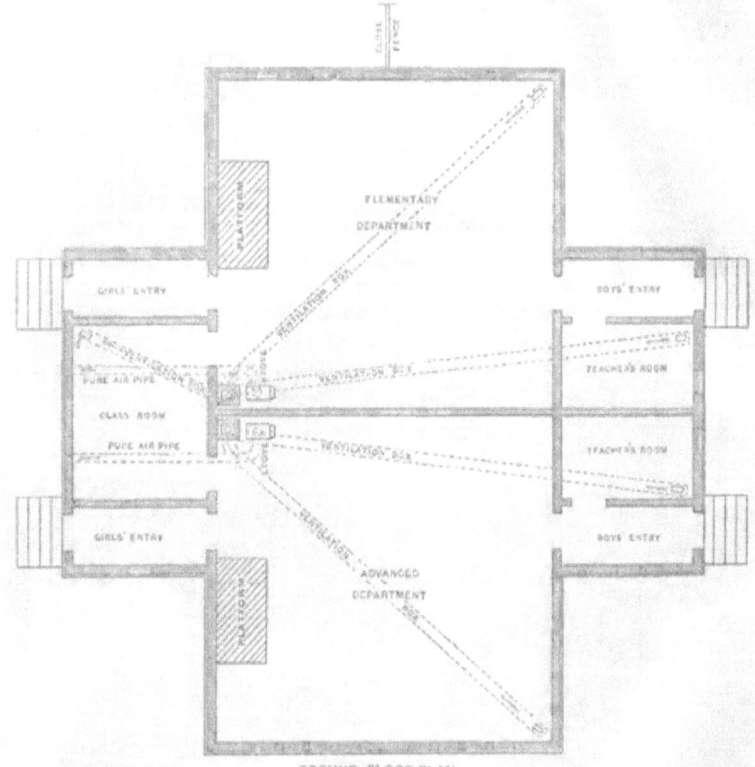

GROUND FLOOR PLAN.
FIG. 52.—FOR A RURAL, OR VILLAGE GRADED SCHOOL.

can be brought **from the** outside of **the** building to the stove (or furnace, if desired). The direction **of the** ventilating flues is also indicated. Teachers' rooms are provided (as marked on the plan), as is also a small class room to the left, **if a kindergarten** is desirable. By adopting this plan, or that of Fig. 45, **provision can** be made, **in** building, for the admission of **light** from only **one side, as** formerly recommended. In that case, the teacher's platform should be so placed **that the** light would come from the left to the **pupils when they are** seated **facing the** teacher.

174. **Fig. 53 gives a section through the centre** of the design and plan, **Figs. 51 and 52. It is intended to show the** interior construction of the

CHAP. XVII.   PLANS FOR RURAL SCHOOL HOUSES.   101

school house, and how the principles of heating, ventilation and lighting, as explained in Chapters XII and XIV. are carried out. The blackboard, it will be seen, extends across the large room, and along the far side of

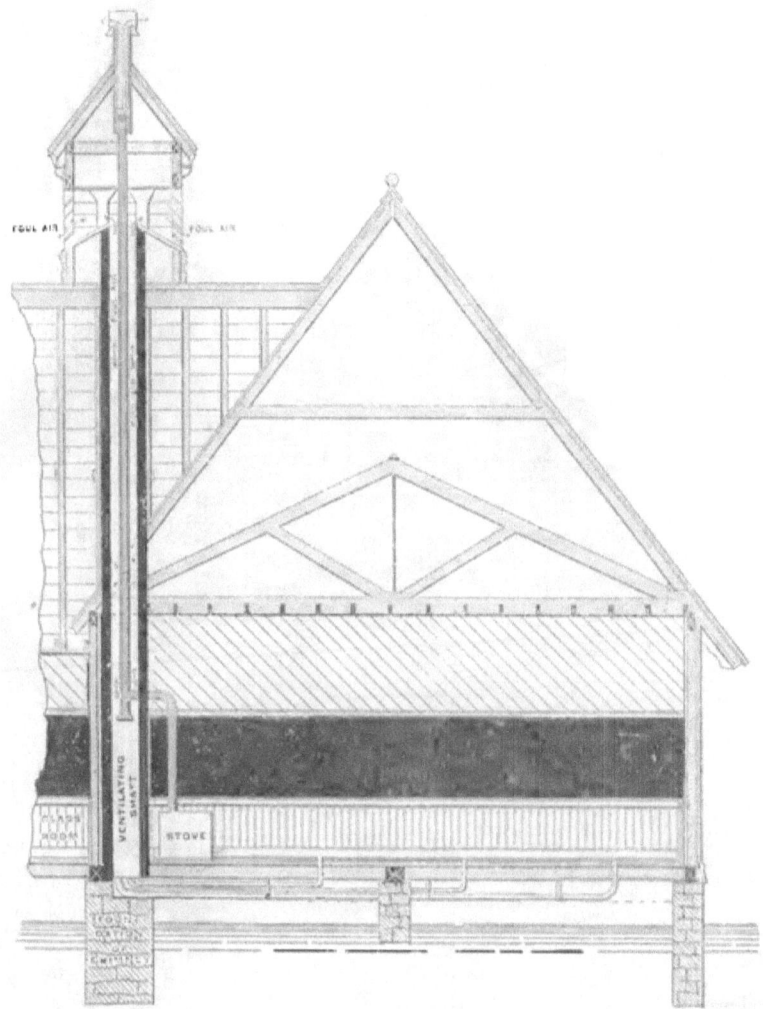

FIG. 53. — SECTION OF THE SCHOOL HOUSE, FIGS. 51 AND 52.

the small class room to the left, in Fig. 52. The upper part of the wall is represented as sheeted diagonally. But this, and the extent of the blackboard, as well as other details, will be at the discretion of Trustees.

175. Fig. 54 is a design for a graded school in a village or town, prepared by Mr. Randell, of Chicago (as indicated in the engraving). It contains two rooms below, and might, by a slight modification, have a third room in the second story (or in the rear) as shown in Fig. 59. Ground

FIG. 54. DESIGN OF A HOUSE FOR A GRADED, RURAL, OR VILLAGE SCHOOL.

plans (Figs. 45 and 55) can be adapted to suit this design. It could also be modified (without altering the position of the entrance doors) so as to form a two story school house, with ground and upper story, as shown in the plans, Figs. 59 and 60.

176. Fig. 55 is another form of a plan for a rural or a village graded school, with but one entrance for girls into the two divisions of the school, and one for boys. The peculiar form of the wardrobe enclosure is a feature of this plan, as is the position of the chimneys and ventilators (shown in the plan at C.C. V.V. V.V.) The position of the stoves is also indicated at S.S. The teachers' platforms are placed so that the light comes to the pupils from the left, as has been before pointed out.

CHAP. XVII.   PLANS FOR RURAL SCHOOL HOUSES.

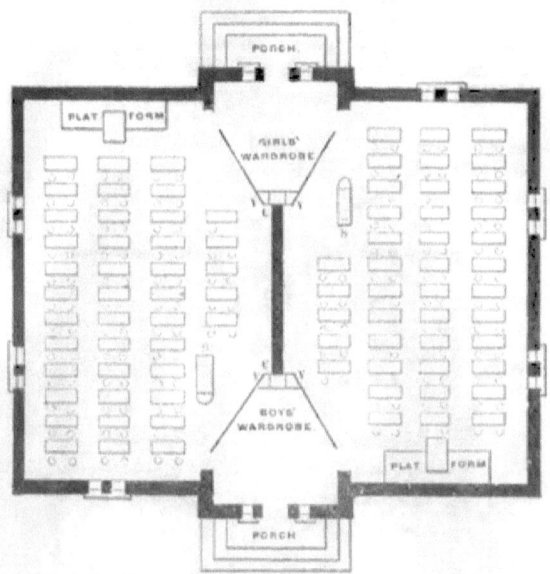

FIG. 55.—GROUND PLAN OF A HOUSE FOR A GRADED RURAL OR VILLAGE SCHOOL.

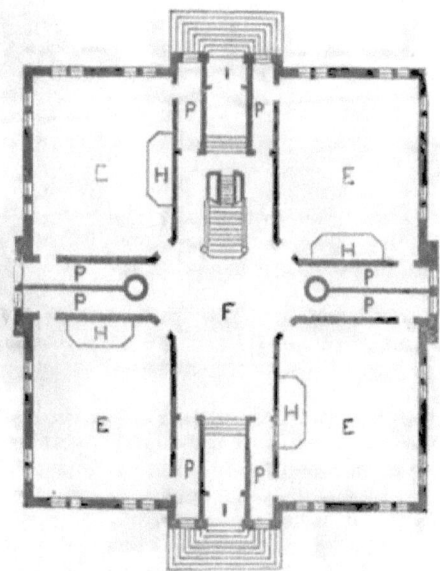

FIG. 56.—GROUND PLAN OF A TWO-STORY SCHOOL HOUSE.

177. Ground plan (Fig. 56) is adapted to design Fig. 54, should it be taken as the basis of one for a two-story school house. The position of the entrance door is the same in both. This plan and that shown in Fig. 57 are those of the Longfellow School House erected in Denver, Colorado (Mr. R. L. Roeschlaud, architect).

178. The plan shown in Fig. 57 is the second or upper floor of the preceding plan (Fig. 56). It differs slightly from it, as the school room is nearly square. Its size is 32 by 33 feet. The teacher's room is over one

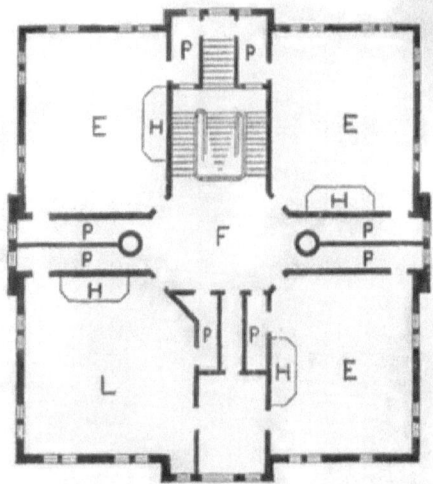

FIG. 57.—UPPER FLOOR OF A TWO-STORY SCHOOL HOUSE.

of the main entrances. These plans can be adapted to designs shown in Figs. 58 and 62.

179. Fig. 58 shows a design for a rural school house, erected at Litchfield, Connecticut. Its outside dimensions **are 30 feet long** by **20 feet wide.** It is of frame, **with** an ornamental **gable.** Cost, $800.

180. The ground plan (Fig. 59) of the Litchfield School House is designed to **seat about 25 or** 30 pupils. The school room is nineteen and a **half (19½) feet square,** with separate **entrances for boys** and girls.

181. Thus, **it will be seen that in the** foregoing illustrations, provision has been made **for giving** practical **effect to** the important suggestions on school **house construction** contained **in the** preceding chapters. Further examples and plans of school houses might be given, but those contained in this chapter are of sufficient variety to enable Trustees to exercise an intelligent choice in regard to the school houses which they may desire to erect—especially in respect to the interior.

CHAP. XVII.   PLANS FOR RURAL SCHOOL HOUSES.   105

FIG. 58.—PLAN OF RURAL SCHOOL HOUSE, LITCHFIELD, CONNECTICUT.

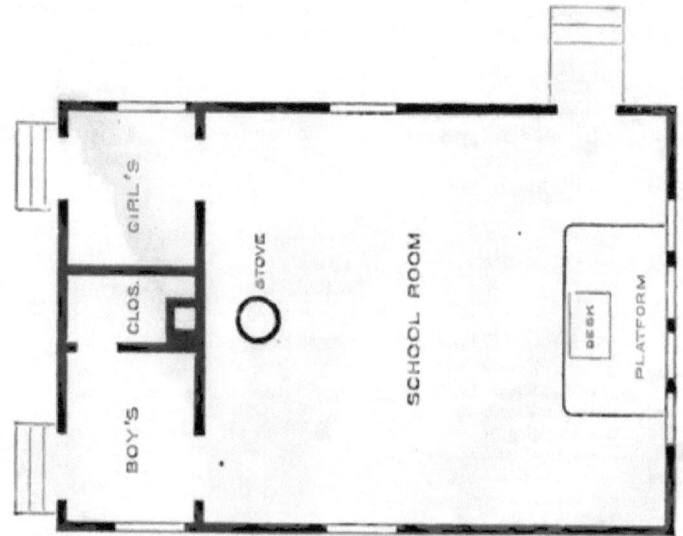

FIG. 59.—GROUND PLAN OF THE RURAL SCHOOL HOUSE, LITCHFIELD.

CHAPTER XVIII.

PLANS FOR SCHOOL HOUSES IN CITIES AND TOWNS.

GENERAL REQUIREMENTS OF SCHOOL HOUSES IN CITIES AND TOWNS.

182. There are a few general principles in the construction of school houses for more than one teacher, which are of special importance, and which should be carefully considered. I have sought to avail myself of the latest experience on this subject.

In the report by Dr. J. D. Philbrick,* issued in 1885 by the Bureau of Education at Washington, he comments on the defects which he had observed in various city school houses in the United States. He also makes several suggestions with a view to the improvement in the construction of school houses of more than one story. I have made a condensed summary of his remarks and suggestions, as follows:

1. *Height.*—A school house should never exceed three stories in height above the basement.† The school rooms, as a rule, should not be placed higher than the second story.

2. *Size.*—A building large enough to accommodate eight hundred pupils should be regarded as the maximum for a school of any grade, whether primary, intermediate, or high. In regard to the size of the primary school house, it would not be far from the mark to say the smaller the number of pupils it accommodates the better for the pupils, provided the number brought together is large enough to admit of a classification. . . . The mammoth school must, from the nature of things, be a second-rate school.

3. *School Furniture.*—The day of hacked seats is gone. It is now well known that nicely made and well polished desks are easily preserved free from injury for many years, even in boys' schools. It is rare to find in our schools the foot rest, which is regarded by eminent foreign authorities as highly important.

4. *Seating.*—[There are two kinds of seats—the single and the double.] The tendency is to substitute the single for the double desk. . . If the desks are not made unnecessarily large, and if they are placed as near

---

* For personal reference to Dr. Philbrick, see note (*) paragraph number 94, page 51.

† Dr Philbrick's preference is for two, instead of three, story school buildings. He says: "A serious, as well as general, fault in the plans of existing school houses is the arrangement requiring too much climbing of stairs, especially in the case of girls. Baltimore, on the other hand, can boast of affording the best examples of the opposite kind. Her high school houses for girls are only two stories high, the study hall being placed in the upper, and the recitation rooms in the lower. A visit to these buildings by Boston school officials, many years ago, induced them to condemn the four story plan of grammar school buildings.

together as convenience will permit, they will require no more space than ought to be allowed, whatever be the mode of seating... The single desk with the separate chair must be regarded as the best mode of seating. The height of the chair and desk should be accurately proportioned to each other, and to the size of the pupils for whom they are intended... There should be at least three sizes of desks and chairs in each room of a graded school... There should be at least six sizes to suit all the grades of an elementary school comprising both the primary and [higher] grades. The chair should be so placed that the front edge of the seat shall be in the same vertical line with the edge of the desk lid.

5. *The Ground Plan.*—If the building is of considerable size, the ground plan should not be in the form of a square, parallelogram, or cross. It should be in L form, or it should be built on three or four sides of a rectangle [with interior courts]. The school house planned after this idea is so far a new departure as to constitute a new type . . —a court type or court plan . This type will, I doubt not, ultimately supersede the type which originated the Quincy school [in Boston, which has been generally followed]. My reason for this opinion is that it has been adopted in those countries where school architecture has been most thoroughly studied, and where the best specimens of school buildings are to be found.

6. *Fire-Proof Roofing.*—In buildings of more than one story in height this important safe guard ought not to be omitted.

7. *Ventilation.*—In the building of the "court" type, having transom windows [as described in paragraph number 94 (3), page 51] and heated by means of indirect radiation, successful ventilation is easily attained.

8. *Orienting.*—Wherever practicable the ground plan of the school should be oriented, that is the corners of the structure should point to the cardinal points of the compass, thus bringing the sides which receive light to face the south-east and north-west and north-east and south-west. This position insures the admission of the sun's rays through every window at some time of the day. In particular, great pains should be taken to prevent, if possible, the facing of unilaterally lighted rooms to the south.

9. *Gymnasium.*—Every city school house of any considerable size should have its gymnasium... It need not be very large; once and one-half the size of the school room might, perhaps, be taken as the minimum size.

10. *Water Closets.*—When detached, this building should be connected with the school house by a covered passage. . . . [See ground plan, Fig. 15, on page 48.]

11. *Entries and Corridors.*—These should be spacious relatively to the stairs, especially at the foot of the latter, and should be lighted directly from out of doors. The lights should be placed at opposite ends, so as to ensure a free, natural ventilation which is the best for entries.

12. *Stairs and Stairways.*—Of these stairs and stairways, Dr. D. F. Lincoln, of Boston, says :—

"They should be isolated, if possible, on at least three sides, by solid brick walls, and should be lighted from outside. The width must be at least six feet in the upper story, and eight in the lower ; and regard must be had that the height of the steps is not too great for children. Spiral stairs are inadmissible, for in such the steps are very narrow near the wall ; and if a child falls the descent is very steep at this point. Wedge-shaped stairs are inadmissible also, for the same reason; and, in turning a corner, they are dangerous. Wells are undesirable, though useful for ventilating the entries. The staircase should be sheathed. Balusters are unnecessary. The rail should be four feet above the riser. Each stairway should have one or two landings, so as to afford a break in the ascent, and a slight resting space."

183. In addition to these important statements and recommendations in regard to school house construction, I add to them other equally valuable and practical suggestions from an American official source.

184. In 1882 a commission (consisting of Dr. John S. Billings, Surgeon in the United States army; Hon. John Eaton, United States Commissioner of Education, and Mr. Edward Clark, architect of the United States Capitol, was appointed by the American Government to report upon the school buildings in the District of Columbia. At the conclusion of their report on the existing school buildings in the District, they make the following recommendations, viz :—

1. "That all sides of the [school] building shall be freely exposed to light and air ; for which purpose they shall not be less than sixty feet distant from any opposite building.

2. "That not more than three of the floors—better only two—shall be occupied for class-rooms.

3. "That in each class-room not less than fifteen square feet of floor area shall be allowed to each pupil.

4. "That in each class-room the window space should not be less than one-fourth of the floor space, and the distance of the desk most remote from the window should not be more than one and one-half times the height of the top of the window from the floor.

5. "That the height of the class-room should never exceed fourteen feet.

6. "That the provisions for ventilation should be such as to provide for each person in a class-room not less than thirty cubic feet of fresh air per minute, which amount must be introduced and thoroughly distributed without creating unpleasant draughts, or causing any two parts of the room to differ in temperature more than 2° Fahrenheit, or the maximum temperature to exceed 70° Fahrenheit. The velocity of the incoming air should not exceed two feet per second at any point where it is liable to strike on the person.

7. "That the heating of the fresh air should be effected by indirect radiation.

8. "That all [wardrobes or] closets for containing clothing or wraps should be thoroughly ventilated."

CHAP. XVIII.   SCHOOL PLANS FOR CITIES AND TOWNS.   109

185. It may be questioned whether these various suggestions have been acted upon in any particular case, as theory and practice do not always agree. Dr. J. D. Philbrick, in his report to Hon. John Eaton, practically solves this question. Speaking of the Vienna Akademisches

FIG. 60.—DESIGN FOR A CITY OR TOWN SCHOOL HOUSE.

Gymnasium, he says, that "it was built . . . as a 'model school,' the design being the product of the best architectural talent and the best pedagogical talent working together. . . . The lighting is perfect. . . . No part of the structure is wider than the combined width of the school room and corridor." Dr. Philbrick also speaks in the highest terms of the Welch Training School, of New Haven, Connecticut. (See paragraph number 199, page 121.

186. School houses in towns and cities are often two or three stories in height. The judgment of the more experienced educators of the present day is in favour of such school houses being only two stories in height, for reasons given in paragraph number 182-1, page 106.

187. Fig. 60 is a handsome design of a school house in Ohio (prepared by Messrs. Randall & Patton, Chicago). It is two stories in height, and

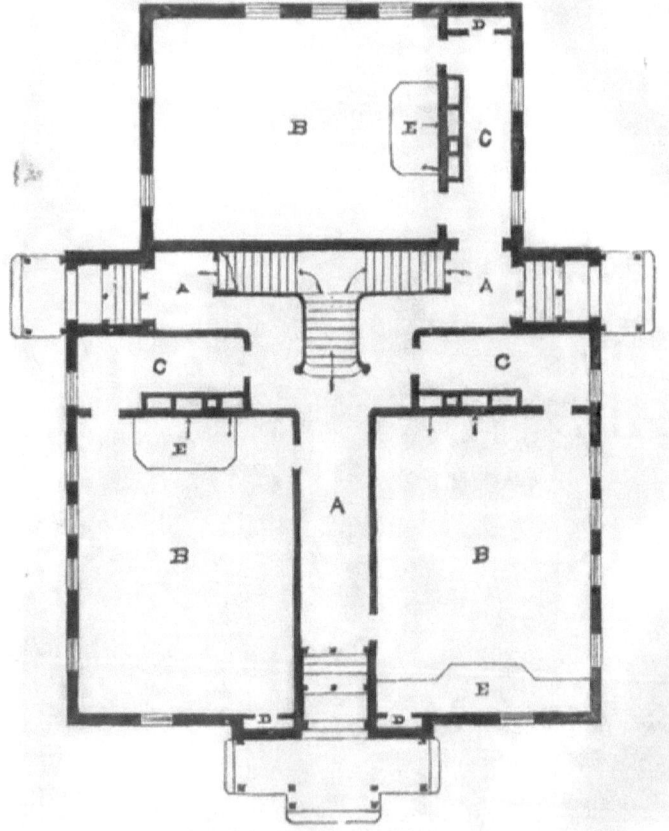

FIG. 61.—GROUND PLAN ADAPTED TO THE FOREGOING DESIGN.

is tastily finished. There is an observatory tower at the top of the building, with railing and canopy. The porch is an open one, which gives a light appearance to the structure.

188. Fig. 61 is the ground plan adapted to this design. There are two rooms in front and one in the rear, with separate entrances for each. Such

Chap. XVIII.   School Plans for Cities and Towns.   111

a building might first be constructed with the two rooms below and two above. Afterwards, the third room in the rear, and one over it might be erected, as the school needed further accommodation. In that case, the part first built should extend far enough to include the outside wall of the stairway to the second floor above, and include the two side entrances A.A. The platforms in the front rooms, B.B., are so placed that the light would

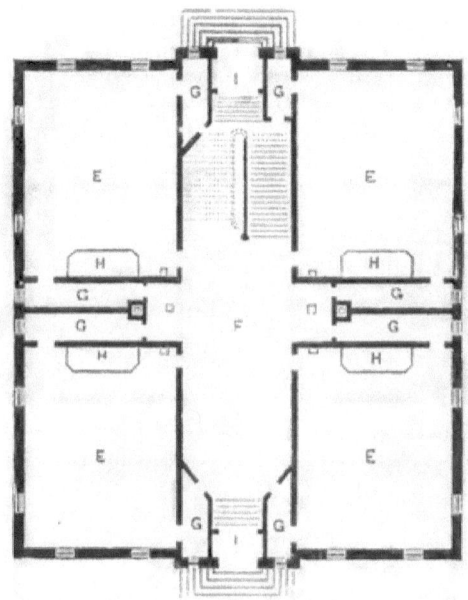

Fig. 62.—Ground Plan of a Two-Story School House.

come in at the left hand side of the pupils in each room. It is suggested that at the outer or entrance doors, the stairs should be in part outside of the doors, and part inside. This is to save expense, as the steps outside should be of stone or other durable material, while those inside may be of wood. The large corridor in the plan, is indicated by the letter A; the teachers' rooms by the letters C.C.C.; teachers' wardrobe by D., and the platforms by E E E. The plan of the second story would, of course, be similarly arranged, and is therefore not given here. See, however, Figs. 65 and 66, which are plans somewhat similar in construction.

189. Fig. 62 is the ground plan of a two-story building—the "Broadway School," erected in Denver, Colorado, and prepared by Mr. R. S. Roeschlaub, architect, and, with other plans, kindly furnished by him. It, with design (Fig. 60), might, if desired, be substituted for the plan (Fig. 61.) The rooms might be small or large, at the discretion of the Trustees. The

plan is a very compact one, and the rooms of which can be easily heated. The following particulars are given by the architect. E E E E, school rooms, each 33 feet by 28 feet; F, central hall, 18 ft. 6 inches wide; G G G G, wardrobes—boys' and girls', for each room; H H H H, platforms;* I I, entrances, 8 feet wide. The registers for hot air are shown in the corners of each school room; and the ventilating flues are seen in the face of the chimneys.

190. Fig. 63 is the plan of the second or upper floor of the school house plan, Fig. 57. The stairs leading up to it in the Denver school, are eight feet wide, with the rise and tread graded to suit the step of children. † The particulars of this floor are as follows:—

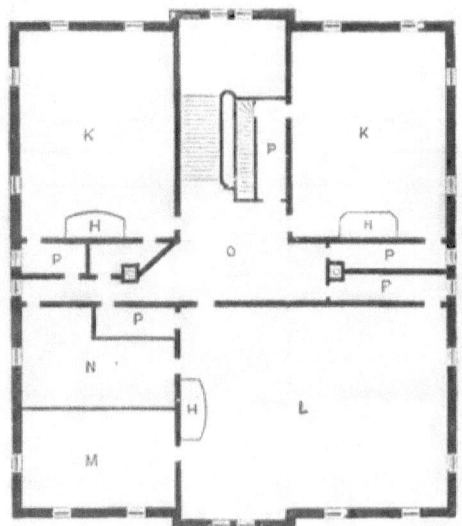

FIG. 63.—UPPER FLOOR OF A TWO STORY SCHOOL HOUSE.

K K school rooms, 28 feet by 33 feet each; L, is a large school, or assembly room, 47 feet by 33 feet; M, class or small recitation room; N, teachers' room; O, the hall; P P P P, wardrobes. The ventilating flues, o o, are shown in the chimneys. These plans are almost identical in arrangement with those shown in Figs. 56 and 57, pages 103 and 104.

---

* Two of these platforms should be differently placed, as is shown in plans (Figs. 45 and 55).

† Too much stress cannot be laid upon this importance of giving every attention to the construction of stairways, and also of the stairs themselves. The former should be wide, and wells should be avoided. The latter should be graded to suit the shortened step of children. The advice on this subject given in paragraphs 180-12, page 108, should, as far as possible, be carefully followed.

CHAP. XVIII.   SCHOOL PLANS FOR CITIES AND TOWNS.   113

191. Fig. 64 is a design for a large school house somewhat in the style of that given in Fig. 60. It was prepared by the same architects. Its general

FIG. 64.—DESIGN FOR A TWO STORY SCHOOL HOUSE.

interior arrangements are similar to those shown in Fig. 61. The modifications are slight, as will be seen on comparing the two designs. The plans of the ground, as well as of the upper or second floor, is given. Both will be found suitable for the interior arrangements of design (Fig. 60). By reference to Fig. 66, the position of the stairs leading up to the second floor will be seen. It differs from that shown in Figs. 56 and 63, and can be otherwise modified, at the pleasure of the school Trustees. Indeed, one principal object had in view, in the insertion of so many "plans" of school houses, was to afford trustees the greatest variety of choice in the

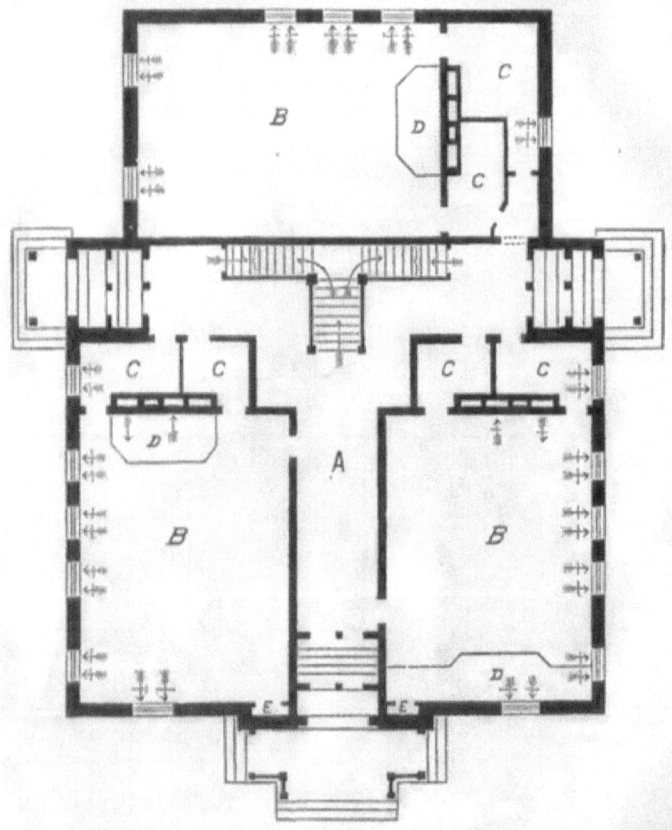

FIG. 65.—GROUND PLAN ADAPTED TO THE FOREGOING DESIGN.

way of interior arrangement. And also to afford them facilities to combine, or alter, these arrangements, as their circumstances might require.

192. The ground plan (Fig. 61) can be adapted to design, Fig. 64, without modification, as they are identical in their general arrangements. The chimneys and ventilating flues are, except in one case, situated in rear of the teachers' platforms. See plans shown in Figs. 65 and 66.

CHAP. XVIII.   SCHOOL PLANS FOR CITIES AND TOWNS.   115

193. It will be seen, on referring to plan, Fig. 66, that great economy of space has been secured in the arrangement of the rooms, both above and below. B B B are the school rooms, and C C C C are designed for small class rooms, teacher's rooms, wardrobes, etc. The teacher's room, or

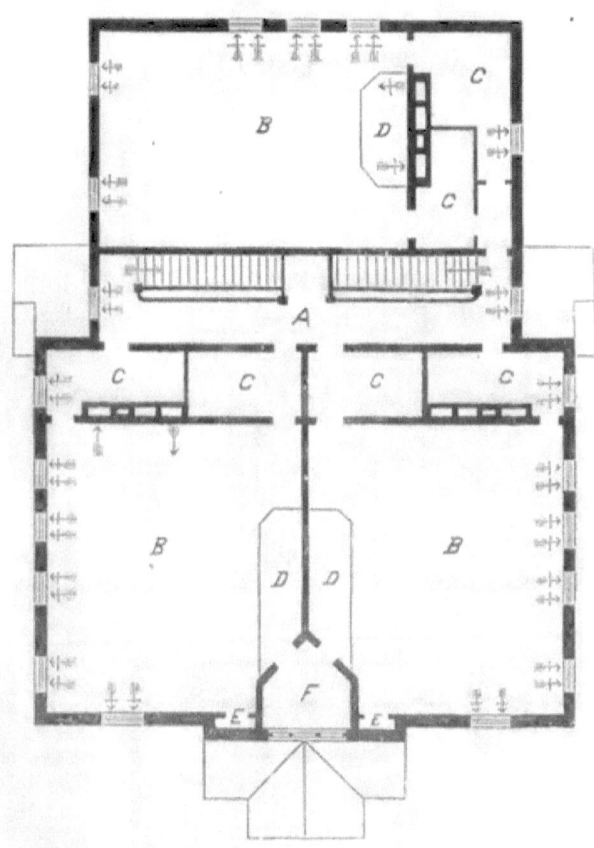

FIG. 66.—PLAN 2, SECOND FLOOR ADAPTED TO DESIGNS 60 AND 64.

library, F in Fig. 66, is ingeniously constructed so as to be of easy access from the teachers' platforms, D D. This room is well lighted by a large window. E E are map and apparatus closets.

194. The ground plan (Fig. 67) can be adapted to the designs (Figs. 60 and 64) by altering the position of the doors. It and the upper floor plan (Fig. 68) are examples (with the others in this book) of different modes of arranging the interior of school houses for cities and towns. It is in this matter of interior arrangement that the greatest difficulty arises. As to the exterior of a school house, that is a matter of taste and of expense; but

the constantly arising demands on School Boards, for increased and improved school accommodation, renders it necessary that the greatest care should be exercised in the planning of the interior of the school building. Economy, convenience, and health have to be consulted, and it is

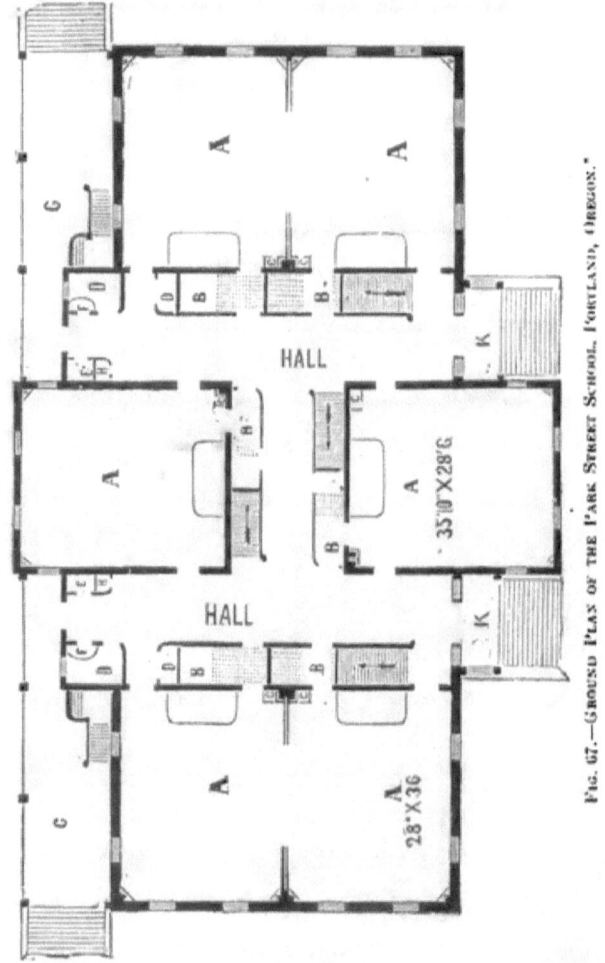

FIG. 67.—GROUND PLAN OF THE PARK STREET SCHOOL, PORTLAND, OREGON."

with a view to aid trustees in this difficult and responsible part of their duty, that I have selected, with the approval of the Minister, and inserted in this book, so many plans of the *interiors* of school houses and but few *exteriors*. There are, however, sufficient of the latter to indicate the pre-

* Explanation of the plan.—A, school room ; B, wardrobe ; C, teacher's closet ; D, book or ap closet; E, hoist; F, lavatory; G, rear porch ; H, hose closet ; K, front porch.

CHAP. XVIII.   SCHOOL PLANS FOR CITIES AND TOWNS.   117

vailing architectural taste of late years in the matter of school houses, especially in the United States. The plans of interiors which have been selected are of very recent date, and have received the approval of those most competent to judge in such matters.

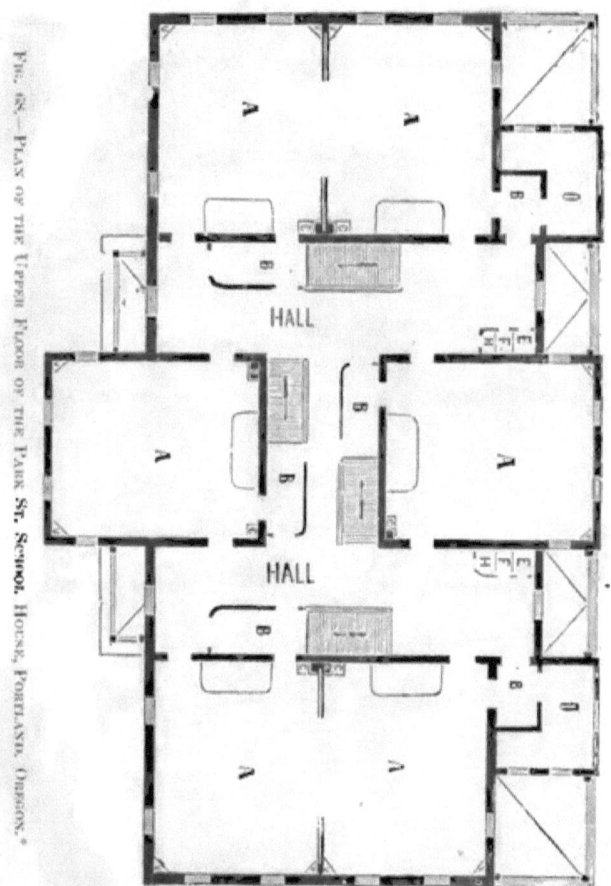

FIG. 68.—PLAN OF THE UPPER FLOOR OF THE PARK ST. SCHOOL HOUSE, PORTLAND, OREGON.*

195. The principal feature to be observed in these plans (Figs. 67 and 68) is the number of means of exit. There are four large entrance doors, giving facilities of easy exit from all of the school rooms. Between the upper and lower floors there are no fewer than four separate stair ways, besides the hoist, so that in case of fire (with the pupils well drilled, as is now required by the Departmental regulations) the school house might be emptied in a very short time.

* Explanation of the Plan.—A, school room; B, wardrobe; C, teacher's closet; E, hoist; F lavatory; H, hose closet; O, teacher's room and library.

118   SCHOOL PLANS FOR CITIES AND TOWNS.   CHAP. XVIII.

196. Fig. 69 is a design of the Whittier school in Denver, Colorado, prepared by Mr. Roeschlaub, architect in that city. It is **147 feet** in length, and **104 feet** deep. From the plan of this interior of the school, and of the Gilpin school in that city (Figs. 67 and 68), it will be seen that ample

FIG. 69.—DESIGN FOR THE WHITTIER SCHOOL HOUSE, DENVER, COLORADO.

space is given for entrance and exit, and for ventilation in each. Dr. John D. Philbrick, in his report, says of these schools :—

" The peculiar merit of the excellent school houses in Denver, is the absence of the . . . common defects of corridors. The Gilpin school house in that city, which I

CHAP. XVIII. SCHOOL PLANS FOR CITIES AND TOWNS. 119

inspected in 1882, two stories high, with six rooms on a floor [Fig. 68], is an admirably specimen of this class. In the Whittier school house, since erected, some further improvements have been introduced. School house building in this wonderful young city has been conducted from the first by the board and superintendent (Mr. A. Gore),

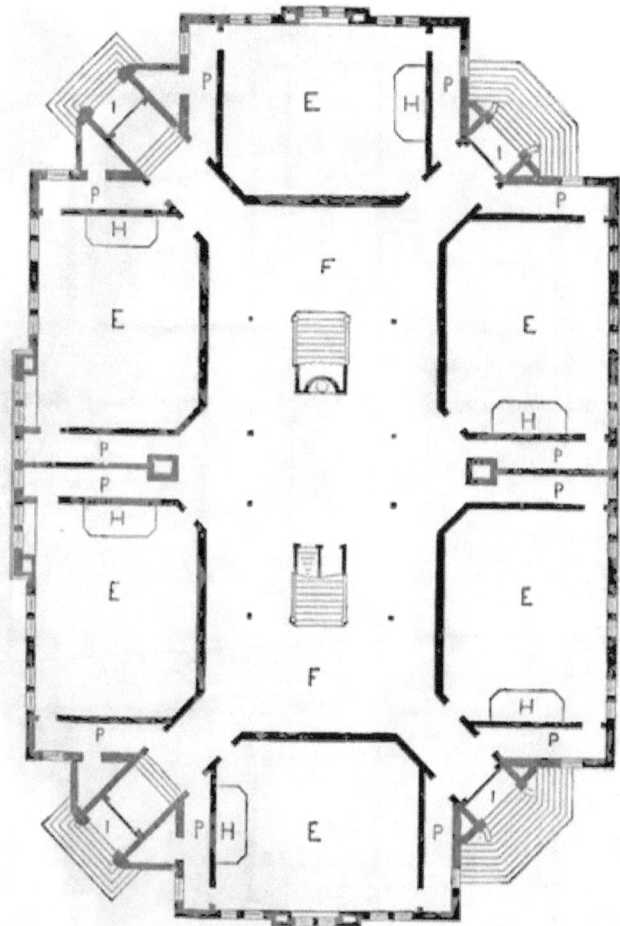

FIG. 70.—GROUND PLAN OF THE WHITTIER SCHOOL, DENVER, COLORADO.

aided by the accomplished architect of the board (Mr. R. S. Roeschlaub), in the most judicious and successful manner, and with the strictest regard to economy, as is evident from the exhaustive report on the subject, published by the board in 1883."

197. The architect gives the following particulars of the ground plan of the Whittier school (Fig. 70), viz. :—

120   SCHOOL PLANS FOR CITIES AND TOWNS.   CHAP. XVIII.

E E, six school rooms, each 28 by 33 feet; F F, corridor, 38 feet 4 in. by 83 feet; H H, **six** teachers' platforms [rightly arranged **for** light]; I I I I, vestibules, **8 feet 7** inches wide ; P P, twelve wardrobes, each 4 ft. 6 inches by 18 feet

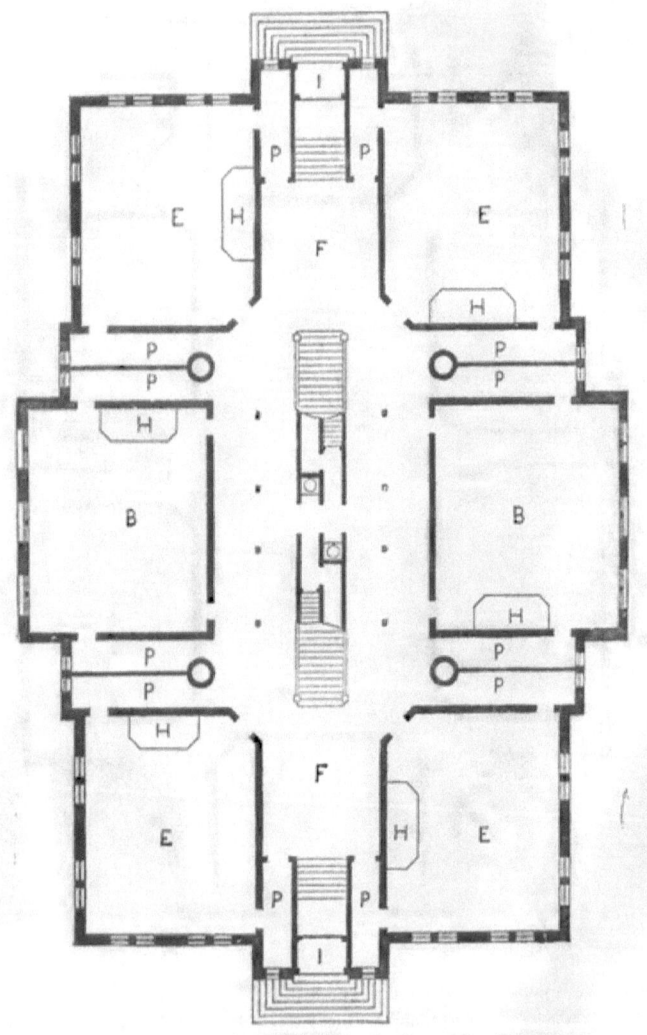

FIG. 71.—GROUND PLAN OF THE GILPIN SCHOOL, DENVER, COLORADO.

198. **The ground plan of** the Gilpin school, Denver, Colorado (Fig. 71), can be easily adapted to the design of Fig. 66. It is, however, defective as

CHAP. XVIII.   SCHOOL PLANS FOR CITIES AND TOWNS.   121

regards "entrances and exits," as compared with the Whittier school, which, as Dr. J. D. Philbrick states, was erected subsequently to the Gilpin school. The particulars of the interior are given by the architect, as follows:

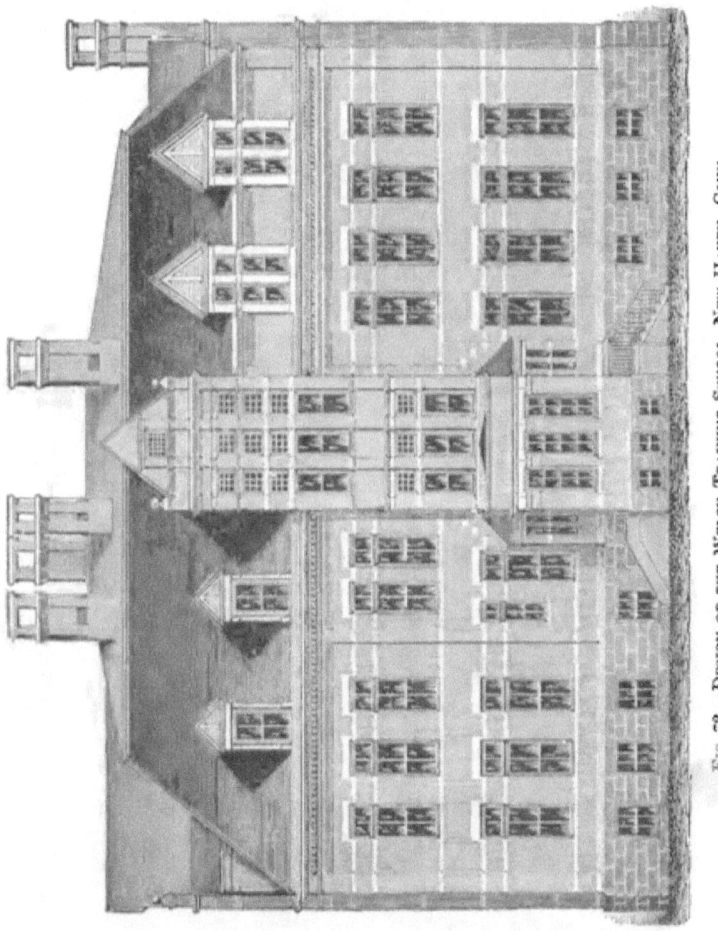

FIG. 72.—DESIGN OF THE WELCH TRAINING SCHOOL, NEW HAVEN, CONN.

B B, school rooms, 28 feet by 33 feet each; E E, four school rooms, each 27 feet by 33 feet; F F, corridors, each 17 feet by 33 feet: H H, teachers' platforms; I I, Vestibules, 7 feet 6 inches wide; P P, twelve wardrobes, each 4 feet 6 inches by 19 feet.

199. Fig. 72 is the design of one of the latest and best planned school houses in the United States. The exterior is plain almost to baldness, and the entrances seem to be small. But the excellence of the building is

in its interior arrangement. The **Secretary** of the Connecticut **State Board** of Education, in his report of **1884**, says:

"In planning the building it has been the aim of the [building] committee to embody all the latest improvements, and features that experience and experts have shown to be of value in school architecture, and especial attention has been given to convenience of plan, lighting, heating, and ventilation, sanitary arrangements and facility of exit. The school rooms are so arranged that the greater part of the light enters the room to the left of the pupils in every case, and the windows extending up to within six inches of the ceiling [See Fig. 40, page 84], admit the light to the opposite

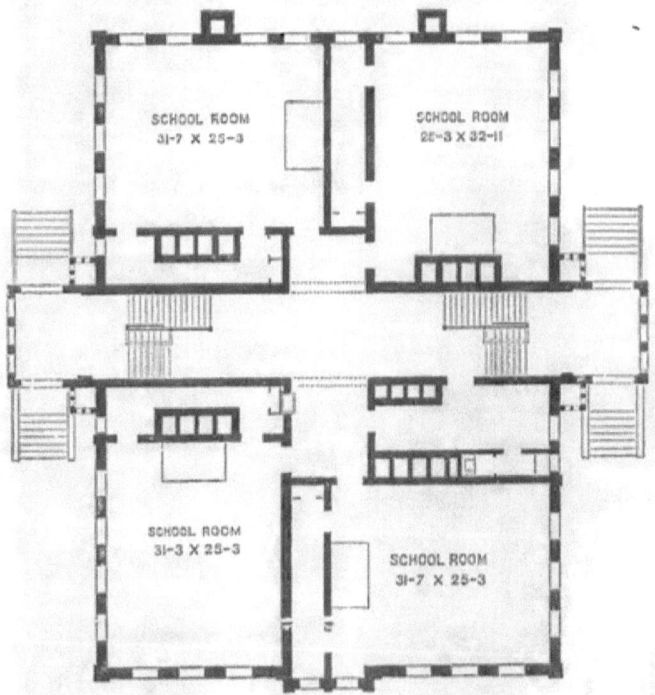

FIG. 73.—GROUND PLAN OF THE WELCH TRAINING SCHOOL, NEW HAVEN, CONN.

side of the room unobstructed. The building is . . . heated throughout by steam, indirect radiation, and in combination with the **system** of ventilation, it is [provided that there shall be] an ample **and** constant flow **of fresh warm air into** every room in the building, in all kinds of **weather.** The steam **coils are** placed at the bottom **of the heating flues** and supplied with fresh air from outside the building through **brick air-ducts, the** outside openings **to these** ducts being some **ten** feet above the ground, so as **to avoid** the possibility of introducing 'ground air' **into** the building. [See paragraph number 123, note page 72.] **The** fresh warm air enters **the** rooms at the height of about seven feet above the floor, and **finds** an egress at **the floor,** after making a **complete circuit, so to** speak, **and** leaves **the** building through **a proper** ventilating **flue.** [See

CHAP. XVIII.   SCHOOL PLANS FOR CITIES AND TOWNS.   123

Figs. 38 and 39.] By this arrangement the air in the rooms will be changed from five to six times an hour during ordinary winter weather. [See paragraph number 109.] It will be seen, then, that we have here a building   .   designed in accordance with the best and most approved principles of school house architecture.   ."

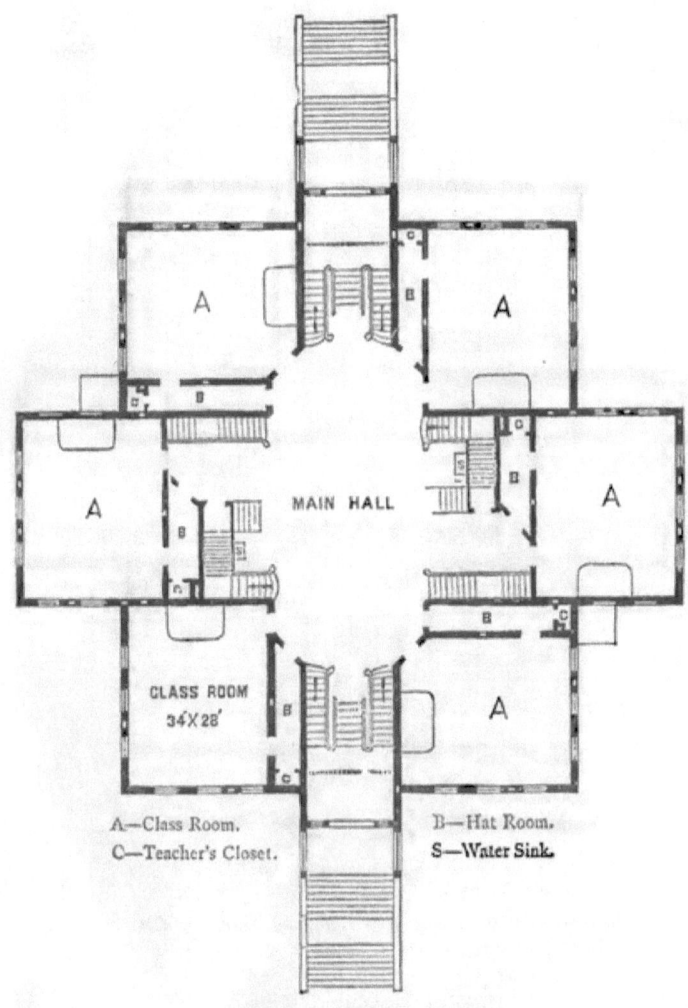

PLAN OF FIRST FLOOR.
FIG. 74.—OF THE COUCH SCHOOL HOUSE, PORTLAND, OREGON.

200. Dr. J. D. Philbrick, in referring to this school house says:

"The school rooms of this building are peculiarly excellent. The length is 31 feet and the width 25 feet. On the long side there are four windows, equally distributed, these windows being at the left of the pupils as seated, and amply sufficient for light. . . . It has two light and airy basement rooms. . . . The system of heating and ventilation is worthy of special attention. . . ."

201. Fig. 74 is the plan of the first floor of the Couch School, erected in Portland, Oregon, in 1883.* This and the plan of the second floor

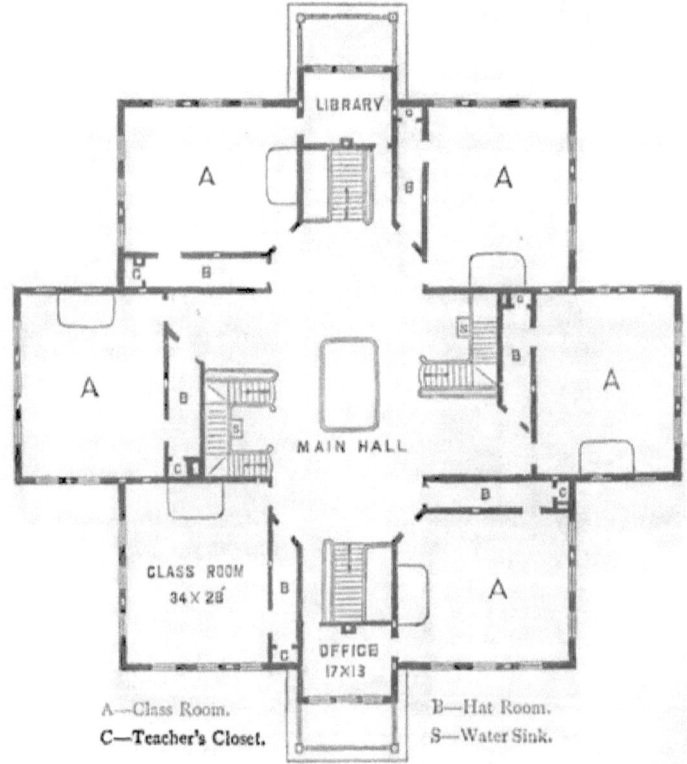

PLAN OF SECOND FLOOR.
FIG. 75.—OF THE COUCH SCHOOL HOUSE, PORTLAND, OREGON.

(Fig. 75) can be easily adapted to designs, Figs. 60 and 64. The chief feature of these plans is the large central or main hall. From it radiate four stair ways leading to the second floor, so as to afford abundant facilities for emptying the school rapidly in case of the alarm of fire. In his report for 1883, Mr. Crawford, referring to this and another school of the same style and arrangement erected at the same time, says:

---

* Mr. J. Krumbein was the architect of this building, and the plans have been kindly furnished by Mr. T. H. Crawford, City Superintendent.

"With scarcely any exception, every appointment and every phase of the arrangement of each building, in reference to light, heat, ventilation, and general conveniences has proven eminently satisfactory. . . The possibility of the complete control over the [pupils of] entire school, as to their movements in the halls and on the stairways has been fully demonstrated."

202. The Superintendent, in another report, gives the following explanation in regard to these plans. He says:

" The extreme length of the main building is 127 feet 8 inches by 116 feet 8 inches. Adding the two porches and stairways to the longitudinal length, the entire depth is 185 feet. . The dimensions of each school room are 34 feet by 28 feet clear, and height of ceiling 16 feet clear. This gives over 15,000 cubic feet of air, or 300 cubic feet to each of 50 pupils. In eight rooms there are six windows, each having an area of actual lighting surface of 36.6 square feet in all. This gives one square foot of light to every 4.3 square feet of floor space. In four rooms there are five windows, giving to each room 183 square feet of window surface, or 1 to 5.2. The standard rate is 1 to 6. All of these rooms, then, are above the standard in respect to light. . . Four flights of stairs lead to the second floor. Those in the main entrance are 4 feet wide, and the second portion 5 feet wide. The side flights are 4 feet 6 inches wide. All the risers are 6⅔ inches high and the treads 11 inches wide. . . The doors to the main entrance are 7 feet wide. Those [in the interior] are 3 feet 3 inches wide and 9 feet high. All doors swing outwards. Transoms 3 feet 3 inches by 2 feet 6 inches are placed over each interior door . . . and have adjustable rods for opening and closing . The bath rooms are practically locked, and can be opened only from the inside. Teachers' platforms are 12 feet by 6 feet 6 inches high."

CHAPTER XIX.

PARTICULARS OF BUILDERS' SPECIFICATIONS.

203. Before entering into a contract for the erection of a school house, specifications for the building should be carefully made out. As these specifications will naturally differ in each case, I can give only the general headings, and a few suggestions as to what should be provided under these headings, viz.:

1. *Excavation.* Specify the size and depth of the excavation for the foundation and the drains, and what shall be done with the excavated earth.

2. *Stone work.* Specify the parts to be built with stone—its kind (cut or rubble); window and door sills, etc., and the quality of the mortar to be used.

3. *Brick work.* Mention the kind of brick, white or red, hard and soft, etc., to be used; the parts to be of brick work; drains and drain pipes. Direct as to the heading course, the bond course, the bed joints, vertical

joints, outside joints, wall facing, and laying the joists and other timber of floor, ceiling, roof, etc.

4. *Lath and Plastering.* Specify what parts shall be lathed and plastered; the kind of lath to be used; furring of walls; quality of plaster and hair; number of coats, and kind of "finish," etc.

5. *Carpenter and Joiner Work.* Kind and size of timber to be used, (as per "bill of particulars" to be made out), common, seasoned, planed and rough, and in what parts each kind is to be used—floor, doors, roof, joists, stairs, windows, and bridging, studding, braces; wainscotings, mouldings, cornices; shingles (sawn or split) if used, or slate. Specify each separately.

6. *Tinwork and Plumbing.* Tin or iron flashing for chimneys, deck, roof, down pipes, eaves, lavatories; joints to be locked and soldered and made water tight.

7. *Hardware.* Mention the kind of quality required of the locks, bolts, hinges, door knobs, sash locks, window weights, transom pivots and catches, clothes hooks, etc.

8. *Painting and Glazing.* Particularize the wood, metal or tin work to be painted; the kind of paint; quality of oil, and the number of coats required; and fire or metallic paint and varnish, and where to be used graining, quality and size of glass; putty; etc.

General Suggestions. Reference should be made in the specifications to the plans and elevation of the building. It should also be required that all work be done and finished in a thorough and workmanlike manner, and with good merchantable materials. A "carpenter's risk" insurance should be provided for, as the building progresses towards completion.

CHAPTER XX.

HINTS ON CONTRACTS WITH BUILDERS.

204. Trustees cannot be too particular in entering into contracts for the erection of a School House. They should see that the plans, elevations, and specifications, as well as the contract itself (in duplicate), are signed by the contractors and their sureties. They should provide for the authorization of extras; by whom and on what conditions. Good and sufficient security should be taken for the performance and completion of the work by a specified time; and a sum, by way of penalty, should be named in the contract for delay in erecting and finishing, the building.

205. As to the law which must govern Trustees in the matter of contracts, I quote the following from my comments and explanation of the "Revised School Law of 1885," published by the Copp-Clark Company, Toronto, last year. In chapter two, section 10, I state that—

"The Trustees alone have the right to decide upon the kind, size, and description of the School House, or Teacher's residence, which they shall erect. No ratepayer, public meeting, or committee has any authority to interfere with or control, them in this matter. They have also full power to decide what fences, outbuildings, sheds, and other accommodations shall be provided. . . To them also exclusively belongs the right to have the school grounds planted with shade trees and properly laid out."

206. As several legal decisions have been given in regard to the contracts and agreements for the erection of school houses, I quote from the work just named the following:—

(1) "*School House Contracts not valid without Trustee Corporate Seal* (Rev. Sch. Act, ss. 25, 104 and 238).—The Court of Common Pleas has decided that school trustees, being a corporation under the school Acts, are not liable, as such, to pay for a school house erected for and accepted by them, not having contracted under seal for the erection of the same. The seal is required as authenticating the concurrence of the whole body corporate. Macaulay, C. J., *dissentiente*.—*Marshall* v. *School Trustees of No. 4, Kitley.* 4 C. P. 373,

NOTE.—Such a contract, not being binding on the corporation, would be binding on the individual trustees who made it with a third party, acting in good faith. *Quære*, whether the trustee-corporation would not, by subsequently taking possession of the school house, or by some other act, recognize the validity of the contract?

2. "*Contract under Seal, signed by a majority of the Corporation, binding* (Ibid).— The same court has also decided the following case:—A contract was entered into by a majority of the trustees, under their corporate seal, for building a school house; after the house was built the trustees refused to pay. In an action brought on the contract, a jury having given a verdict in favor of the trustees on a plea of *non est factum*, a new trial was ordered, and the former verdict in favor of the trustees set aside. The court *held* that a contract entered into by a majority of the trustees under the School Act, with the corporate seal attached, is sufficient; and a plea that the contract was signed by the subscribing trustees, without the consent or approbation of the others, was *held* bad.—*Forbes* v. *School Trustees of No. 8, Plympton.* 8 C. P. 73, 74.

3. "*Arrangements under seal for building school house, although indefinite, was binding upon the parties.*—The agreement sued on was headed, 'Specification of School House in School Section No. 4, Tilbury East.' Then followed in detail the size of the building, and the work and material to be employed, and it concluded: 'The whole to be of good material, and to be finished in a good workmanlike manner, and to be finished on the 1st of July, 1873. In consideration the parties of the first part agree to pay the party of the second part the sum of $708, one-half on the 15th May, and the other half when the school house is completed.' Then followed the signatures of the three school trustees, with their corporate seal, and the signature of the plaintiff. It bore no date, but was proved to have been executed by the parties about the 1st March, 1873. It referred to no plan, but the trustees furnished the plaintiff with a plan to work by, and they paid to him $400 on account. They refused to pay the balance, or to accept the building, alleging that it was not properly constructed; but the learned Queen's Counsel, who tried the case without a jury, found for the plaintiff for the balance of the $708. *Held*, that it was sufficiently clear from the instrument itself and the acts of the parties that defendants were the parties covenanting with the plaintiff, and that the instrument was intended so to operate, and the verdict was upheld.— *Coghlan* v. *The School Trustees of S. S. No. 4, in the Township of Tilbury East, in the County of Kent*, 35 Q. B. 575.

4. "*School house and site in use not liable to be sold on judgment against Trustee-Corporation.*—The Court of Queen's Bench has given judgment as follows :—In a case in which a school site had been given to the trustees for the purposes of a school (with the condition that it should revert to the giver in case it should cease to be used for school purposes), and on which they had erected a school house, judgment was obtained against the corporation for the money due on the building contract. The school house and site were actually sold and deeded by the sheriff; but the court held that the house and land could not lawfully be sold—it being contrary to public policy that a school house in daily use (any more than a court house or jail) should be held liable upon a writ of execution, as not the trustees, but the inhabitants of the locality, are the *cestuis que trust* (*i.e.*, the persons for whose benefit the trust is held). The plaintiff should have resorted to his other remedies against the trustees for neglect of duty.—*Scott* v. *Trustees of Union section No. 1 Burgess and 2 Bathurst*, 19 Q. B. 28.

5. "*Proposed School House—Submission to electors.*—It appeared from the affidavit of the secretary-treasurer of a school section that at two regularly called meetings of the duly qualified electors of a school section, at which a chairman was appointed, proposals to borrow money for the purchase of a site, and build a school house, were put by way of motions, and carried, upon which a by-law was passed authorizing the issue of debentures to raise money for the above purposes. *Held* by Armour, J., that under the School Act cited this was a sufficient submission to, and approval of, the proposal by the duly qualified electors, and a rule to quash the by-law was discharged.—*In re McCormick and the Corporation of the Township of Colchester South.* C. L. S. I. 215.

6. "*Note.* The Assessment Act exempts from taxation 'every public school house with the land attached thereto and the personal property belonging to it.'"

INDEX.

	Page.
Accommodation, School, Regulations regarding	7
Acid, Carbolic—*see* Carbolic Acid.	
Carbonic acid—*see* Carbonic Acid.	
Age of Pupils, and size of Seats and Desks	8, 86
Air Brick, Jennings	85
Chamber in Ventilation	73
Cubic feet of, per Child	8, 12, 50, 64, 67
Currents in a School Room	62, 73, 85
Evils of bad	11, 12, 13, 70
For Children, how much	8, 12, 50, 64, 71, 74
Heating by hot	67, 71, 72
Inlets in Windows	62, 70, 71
See Inlets and Outlets.	
Akademisches Gymnasium, Vienna	67, 109
Albany Schools, N. Y., School Authorities quoted	74, 76, 77
Albuminoid Ammonia defined	25
American Council of Education quoted	78
Ammonia Albuminoid	25
Free	25
Artificial Ventilation and Natural	60, 63
Ash System for Privies	27, 35, 36
Trees for Shade	40
Bacillus and their spores	37
Bacteria, what they are	22
Balusters in Staircases unnecessary	108
Baltimore High School for Girls	106
Barnard, Dr. Henry, Hartford, Connecticut	66
Battens for Matched Boards, Patterns for	99
Beam, a notched	58
Berlin Schools, Germany	66
Billings, Dr. John S., Washington	108
Blackboards, Brushes for, how made	60
Directions for making	9, 59, 60
In Schools	51, 59, 60, 81
Regulations regarding	9
Blinds for Windows	83
Block Plan of School Grounds	48, 49
Bond of School House Wall	57, 58
Boston Schools, Massachusetts	66, 67
Movement for School Room Decoration	91
Brick, Air, Jennings	85
Bridgeport Schools, Connecticut	67, 80
Briggs, W. R., Architect, Connecticut	69, 80
Brown, Hon. Le Roy, Ohio	95
Brimstone as a Disinfectant	37

	Page.
Brushes for Blackboards, how made	60
Brussells Educational Congress	50, 52, 79
Bryce, Dr. P. H., quoted	21, 22, 24, 70
Builders, Contracts with	126
Specifications	125
Building, Details of School	52, 106
Buisson, Director of French Primary Education	90
Buk, Dr., quoted	81
Burrows, F., Napanee, quoted	30, 69
Butcher, Hon. B. L., West Virginia	39
Carbolic Acid as a Disinfectant	37
Carbonic Acid, Exhalation of	65
Cesspool for Lavatories	32
Plan of	33
Chalk, Trays for Blackboards	59
Chamber, Air, in Ventilation	73
Chestnut Trees for Shade	40
Chicago, School Recess in	79
Chloride of Zinc, Solution of	37
Lime	37
Cincinnati, School Recess in	78
Cities and Towns, Plans for School Houses in	106
Clark, T. M.—see United States Book, etc.	
Edward, quoted	108
Clematis in School Grounds	42
Cloak rooms in School Houses	46
See Wardrobes	
Closets, Dry Earth	27
Clothes	46, 52
Clothes Closets in Schools	52
See Wardrobes.	
Congress, Educational, at Brussells	50
Connecticut Normal School, Principal	51
Reports of School Board of, quoted	80
Secretary, quoted	122
Construction of School Houses	50, 52
Consumption (phthisis) in Schools	13
Death of Female Teachers, from	11
Contracts with Builders	126
Copperas as a Disinfectant	37
Cornice of School Houses	55, 56, 57
Corridors in Schools	107
Cost of School Houses	67
Cottier System of Ventilation	73
Couch School, Portland, Oregon	123, 124
Covernton, Dr. C. W., quoted	58
Crawford, T. H., quoted	77, 122, 124
Crookshank, A. S., on Fire, Escape, Drill	75
Cubic Feet of Air per Child	8, 12, 50, 64, 67
Currents of Air in a School Room	62, 73, 85
Dayton, Ohio, School Recess in	79
Dearness, John, quoted	11, 14, 23, 61, 69, 80
Decoration of School Rooms	88, 92
Denver, Colorado, Schools in	104, 111, 118, 120

INDEX.

	Page.
Deodorizers	36
Desks and Seats in Schools, Position of	51
Regulations regarding	8, 85
Single, approved	8, 50
Diphtheria and Typhoid Fever in Schools	12
Diseases, School Room	12, 80
Disinfectants	36
Disinfection	36
Dog-Tooth Ornament	57
Donovan, C., quoted	69
Doors of School Houses	51, 75
Downs, Hon. C. A., New Hampshire, quoted	20, 22, 24
Drainage, from Privy Pit, to Well	21
of School Grounds	14
Drill, Fire, in Schools	74
Dry Ash System	27, 35
Earth System	27, 33
Earth Closets, Dry	27, 34
Eaton, Hon. John, reference to	14, 39, 41, 50, 51, 108, 109
Educational Congress, Brussells	50
Association, United States	50
Elms as Shade Trees	40
English Committee on School Room Decoration	91, 92
Entrances, Separate, to School Houses	45, 106
to Open Outwards	46
Escape, Fire Drill	74, 75
Evergreens as Shade Trees	41
Evils Preventable	17
of Bad Air	11, 12, 13
Exit from School Houses, ready	74
Female Teachers, Death of, by Consumption	11
Fences and School Entrances	44
Filters, Defective	22
Fire, Danger of, from Furred Walls	54
Drill, in Schools	46, 74, 75
Roofing	107
Floor Space per Pupil—*see* Cubic Feet, etc.	
and Window Space	108
Floors in School Rooms	58
Flowers in School Grounds	17, 42, 43, 47, 88
" " Rooms	88
Flues, Ventilation	63
Forchammer's Test for Water	24
Forestry in Ontario	40
the United States	42
Fotheringham, David, quoted	11, 30, 67, 71
Foundation of School Houses	52, 53
Fox, on Air and Water	70
French Authorities on Lighting School Houses	74
Commission on School Room Decorations	90
System of Seating Pupils	88
Furnaces in Schools	68, 71
Furniture, School, Regulations regarding	8, 106
Furred Walls, Dangerous	54

	Page.
Gates to School Grounds,	44, 45
German Commission on **School Hygiene**	74
Germany, Lighting School **Houses in**	80, 82
Girls, Privies, or Latrines **for**	28, 29
Gilpin **School**, Denver, Colorado,	120
Glass, **Window, per Pupil**	81
Globes, **Regulations** in **regard to** Schools,	9
Grounds, School, Plan of,	47, 48, 49, 107
and Play Shed	38
Hamilton, Hess St. School, in,	75
Hancock, Dr. John, quoted,	78
Harris, Dr. W. T., quoted,	50, 78
Harrison, E. B., quoted,	69
Health, Board of, National, **United States**	22
New Hampshire,	17, 20, 22, 36, 37
New York,	25, 37, 46
Provincial (Ontario),	10, 12, 17, 31, 35, 37, 64, 77, 80, 84
of Children in Schools,	50
Heating and Ventilation of School Houses,	60, 67, 71
Height of Class Rooms,	108
School Houses,	106, 108
Hess Street School, **Hamilton**,	75
Hopkins University, Johns—*see* **University**,	
Hot Air, Heating by,	67, 68, 69, 71, 72
Hough, Dr. F. B., quoted,	41, 42, 43
Houses, School, Construction of,	50
Position of,	51
Regulations regarding,	7
Howland, George, quoted,	78
Hygiene, Work on School,	88
Hygienic Conditions of School House Construction,	50
Value of the School Recess,	76
Inlets and **Outlets of** Air in School **Rooms**,	62, 70, 71
Inspection of Schools, Medical,	50
Intermission, School—*see* Recess,	
Iowa's School Motto,	13
Iron, Sulphate **of, as a Disinfectant**,	37
Jenning's Air Brick	85
Johonnot, J., quoted,	16
Johns Hopkins University	37
Larches as Shade Trees,	41
Latrine—*see* Privy,	
Lavatories, Construction of,	32
Leeds, Professor, quoted,	70
Left side of Pupils, Light from the—*see* Lighting,	
Lighting School Houses,	45, 50, 51, 79
Lime, Chloride of, as a Disinfectant,	37
Lincoln, Dr. D. F., quoted,	31, 46, 62, 63, 71, 72, 77, 108
Lindens as Shade Trees,	40
Linell, Dr., quoted	80
Liquid Slating for Blackboards,	60
London, City of, England, School of, Described,	67

INDEX.

	Page
Maples as Shade Trees	40, 41
Maps, School, Regulations, regarding	9
Medical Commission, German, on School Hygiene	74
Inspection of Schools	50, 75
Michigan State School Superintendent, quoted	81
Myopia in Schools	80, 81
McBrien, James, quoted	30
New Brunswick Plan of School Grounds	49
Privy Construction	28, 30
England Journal of Education, quoted	92
Hampshire Board of Health	17, 20, 22, 36
Haven School, Connecticut	110, 121
York City, Prize School Plans	67
School Room, Decoration in	89
State Board of Health	25, 35, 46, 62, 72
Nichols, Dr. J. R., quoted	12
Northrop, Hon. B. G., quoted	39
Oaks as Shade Trees	40
Oldright, Dr., quoted	22, 70, 75, 84, 85, 87, 88
Ontario Board of Health—see Board of Health.	
Opening Doors Outwards	51, 75
Oregon, Schools in Portland	73, 77, 116, 123
Organic Impurities in Water	23
Orienting School Houses	107
Outlets of Air—see Inlets.	
Panelling in School Rooms	59
Peaslee, Dr. J. B.	39
Percolation from Privy, Pit, to Well	21
Permanganate of Potash	36
Test	23, 24, 25
Philbrick, Hon. Dr. J. D., quoted	50, 51, 52, 66, 67, 74, 78, 79, 81, 87, 89, 96, 106, 109, 118, 121
Phipps, R. W., quoted	40
Pines as Shade Trees	41
Pittsburgh, School Room Decoration in	89
Plans for Privies	27
of School Houses in Cities and Towns	106
Rural Sections	93
Planting Shade Trees, Time for	40, 42
Plaster Casts in Schools	89
Play Grounds and Sheds	38, 39, 48, 49
Plastering—see Specifications.	
Porches to School Houses	45, 46
Portland, Oregon, Schools in	73, 77, 116, 123
Primary School Houses	51, 93
Privies, Ash Pail System for	27
Construction of	25, 26
Dry Earth System for	27
How They should be managed	26
Plans for	27, 48, 49
Seat for	27
Privy Pit Drainage towards Well	21
Provincial Board of Health—see Health.	
Pulleys, Windows without	84
Pumps in School Grounds	47

	Page
Randall and Pattou, Architects, Chicago	102, 110
Reasons for the Publication of this Book	10
Recess, School, Hygienic Value of	66, 96
Reflected Light in School Rooms	74, 81, 84
Rickoff, Hon. A. J., quoted	80
Risers and Treads in Stairs	108
Robson, quoted	80
Rochester, New York, Schools, Fire, Drill in	75
Roeschlaub, R. L., reference to	104, 111, 119
Roofing, Fire, for School Houses	107
Room, a Model School	51
Decoration, School	88
Roses in School Grounds	42
Rural School House Plans	93
Ruskin, John, on School Room Decoration	89
Sanitary Inspection of Schools—*see* Medical.	
Sashes, Window	56, 61, 81, 83, 84
School House, Position of	51
Seating School Rooms	8, 50, 51, 85, 87, 106
Seats, Privy, Construction of	27
Regulations regarding	8, 85
Separate Entrances for Boys and Girls	45, 46, 107
Shade Trees in School Grounds	39
Sheds, Plan of, and Play Ground	83
Sheringham Valve	85
Shrubs in School Grounds	42
Sill, a Notched	58
Window	83, 84
Construction of	37
Site, School, Regulations regarding	7, 13
Selection of a School	13, 14
Size of	47
Size and Shape of School Room	51, 66, 67, 105
Slating Liquid, for Blackboards	60
for Urinals	31
Smith, Dr. A., Test for Water Impurity	70
Southern Aspect for a School House	14
Specifications for Builders	125
Stairs, Broad, recommended	75, 108
Stoves in Schools	67, 69, 71, 72
Sulphate of Iron	37
Sulphur as a Disinfectant	37
Summerby, W. J., quoted	69
Teachers' Association of Ontario	30
Female, Death of, from Consumption	11
Tests for Impurities in Water	18, 23, 24
Air	70
Forchammer's, for Water	24
Permanganate for Water	23
Tidy's, for Water	24
Tidy's Test for Water	24
Tobin's Tubes	85
Transom Lights over Doors	61
Trap System for Privies	27
Treads and Risers in Stairways	108
Trees, Shade, in School Grounds	39, 40
Time for Planting Shade	40

	Page.
Tronnisdorf, quoted	25
Tubes—see Tobin.	
Typhoid Fever and Diphtheria in Schools	12
Unilateral Principle of Lighting	74, 81
United States, Book on School Architecture	26, 28, 30, 31, 32, 38, 42, 43, 45, 46, 53, 60, 66, 82, 86, 99
Commission on School Houses, D. C.	79
National Board of Health	22
University of Johns Hopkins	37
Urinals for Boys	28, 31
Valve, Sheringham	85
Vaults, Privy, Construction of	27, 28, 30
Ventilation and Heating of School Houses	60, 67, 107, 108
by Means of Windows	56, 61, 84
Natural and Artificial	60
Vestibules in School Houses	46, 59
Vienna Schools	67, 75
Exposition	66
Village School House Plans	93 to 106
Virginia Creeper in School Grounds	42
Wadsworth, Dr. J. J., quoted	30
Wainscoting, Kind of	58
Wanklyn, quoted	25
Waller, Dr., quoted	24
Walls, Bond for Outside	57, 58
Furred, Dangerous	54
of School Houses	51, 54
Wardrobes in School Houses	46, 52, 108
Washbowls in Schools	47
See Lavatories.	
Water Closets—see Privies.	
Constituents of	24, 25
Evil Effects of Polluted	18, 22
Test for Pure	18, 24
Welch Training School, New Haven, Connecticut	110, 121
Well in School Grounds	17, 18
Percolation to, from Privy Pits	21
Wells in Staircases Undesirable	108
Whittier School, Denver, Colorado	118
Wilson, Dr. George, quoted	65
Window Blinds	83
Sash	56, 66, 81, 83
Space, and Floor Space	108
Windows in School Rooms, Construction of	50, 51, 56, 61, 79, 82
Ventilation, by means of	66
Without Pulleys	84
Wisconsin State Superintendent, quoted	15, 29, 38, 42, 43, 44, 45
Plan of Privies for Girls	28, 29
Woods, Collection of Native	43
Wood-shed, Construction of	37
Workman, Dr., quoted	11
Yards, Play	39
Yeoman, Dr., H. P., quoted	13, 77
Zinc, Solution of Chloride of	37

www.ingramcontent.com/pod-product-compliance
Lightning Source LLC
Chambersburg PA
CBHW020104170426
43199CB00009B/385